WITHDRAWN

STITCH
IN
TIME

STITCH
IN
TIME

BY JOHN GOULD

Illustrations by Consuelo Eames Hanks

W·W·NORTON & COMPANY

NEW YORK   LONDON

Published simultaneously in Canada by
Penguin Books Canada Ltd.
2801 John Street, Markham, Ontaro L3R 1B4.
Printed in the United States of America.

The text of this book is composed in Palatino,
with display type set in Palatino.
Composition and Manufacturing by
The Maple-Vail Book Manufacturing Group.

First Edition

Library of Congress Cataloging in Publication Data

Gould, John, 1908–
Stitch in time.

1. Gould, John, 1908–   —Biography.   2. Authors,
American—20th century—Biography.   I. Title.
PS3513.0852Z474   1985   818' 5209 [B]   84–22599

ISBN 0-393-01976-4

W. W. Norton & Company, Inc.
500 Fifth Avenue, New York, N.Y. 10110
W. W. Norton & Company Ltd.
37 Great Russell Street, London WC1B 3NU

1 2 3 4 5 6 7 8 9 0

In Memory of
Robert H. McCauley, Jr.,
and to his wife, Lois.

Contents

CONTENTS

Peter Partout's Page

Dear Mr. Editor: Mrs. Partout read this book before publication, and I think her opinion is all right. She said:

> "Dr. Gould's gentle prose soothes and pleases me. His quiet fun is charming. His grammar and syntax precise, his selection of words amazing, his alliterative passages perfect, his allegory and metaphor delightful, and in every way I consider him our best master of the personal essay. He never abuses my finer sensitivities. Which is fine, because so many other writers these days make me want to puke."

(Signed) Peter Partout

Peppermint Corner, Maine

Venienti occurrite morbo.
Persius Flaccus
A stitch in time saves nine.
Proverb

Where it Started . . .

Legend, not always reliable, says the poker game at the Adelman Brothers potato warehouse at Mars Hill, up in Aroostook County, Maine 04758, never ceases. If somebody excuses himself, somebody else sits in and the play goes on day and night. One morning the pot was right and Heem Blodgett was contemplating his pair of queens. Freddie Manter walked in and handed out the cigars.

"Nine and a half pound boy!" he announced.

"Big baby!" said Leslie Dunbar.

Freddie says, "Eyah—Doc had to take nine stitches!"

"Nine stitches!" says Heem. "Migod, Freddie, only takes six stitches to close a potato bag!"

STITCH
IN
TIME

Talk About Stitching!

My wife was lately drawn for jury duty, thus becoming an expert on jurisprudence, and when the notice came it had a questionnaire with it so she could set down her qualifications, and also her willingness. She responded that she was more than willing to perform this civic duty, so off she went each morning, my lonely noontime sandwich cooling in the refrigerator. But she would soon be home again, sometimes before I had finished my sandwich, and she would lament that the lawyers passed her by. Day after day, case after case. I suggested she take the Dale Carnegie course and make herself more popular. For each attendance at the courthouse the county paid her a stipend established by the legislature in 1820, and we figured that on top of that it was costing us thirty-six dollars a day to support Law and Order. Then, one day, she stayed all day and came home happy. She had served. The lawyer for the defense had manfully made his plea, but the decision was unanimous—guilty. On that note she was dismissed, and I began getting hot lunches again.

Now, here's the real story:

Raoul Livernois and Roger Duplessis were members of two significant bodies—the City Council and the Club Rouge et Noir. The Club Rouge et Noir was a social society, a licensed drinking establishment where members could buy booze for less than at a pub and drink it in the company of congenial friends. Sometimes Raoul and Roger would visit the club on other nights, but they always went there after the City Council meetings on

Wednesday nights. On the eventful evening now in focus, after City Council meeting, they arrived at the club in Raoul's automobile, Raoul driving, and they had maybe t'ree-four. Ready to go home, they paid up and got into Raoul's automobile, Raoul driving, and shortly the erratic progress of the vehicle drew the attention of Officers Benoit and Caron, in a police cruiser. When the flashing lights of the cruiser were turned on, Raoul pulled over to the curb, and Roger said, "Quick! Shift places! I know these cops and can fix things!"

So they shifted places and Roger was now behind the wheel. He ran down the window and smiled pleasantly at the approaching Officer Benoit. But it was not Officer Benoit. It was a rookie policeman, and Roger didn't know him from a crock of Morse's sauerkraut. The consequence was that Roger, who was not the driver, was ordered into court on a charge of driving under the influence.

Raoul, who had been the driver, wasn't charged with anything, and he felt truly sorry at the way things had turned out. "Get a lawyer," he told Roger, "and have him continue the case."

Of course, when Roger found a lawyer, he didn't tell him anything about changing places. The lawyer told Roger the case wasn't important enough to matter—to go and plead nolo and pay the fine. It costs money to continue a case, he said. Which makes sense, because the lawyer didn't know that Roger was innocent. Raoul told Roger, "Don't do it. Continue the case. Everything's going to work out!"

Meantime my wife was drawn for jury duty, and now Raoul came to Roger and said, "Go into court next Monday. Everything's going to be all right." So, shrugging his shoulders, the lawyer went to court with Roger on that Monday, and entered a plea of not guilty for him, and sat back to listen to the testimony of the rookie policeman. He told how the progress of the vehicle was erratic enough to attract attention, that it was being operated in a manner to endanger, that the operator was unquestionably under the influence, and that he had arrested him. The operator was, he pointed, the respondent.

Roger's lawyer offered a feeble defense, but shrugged his shoulders again as he sat down. But Roger smiled knowingly, and well he might—because Raoul was sitting up in the jury box beside my wife and, as he had said, everything was going to work out.

The jury didn't take much time. My wife said one juror asked, "Why would a lawyer take a thing like that into court anyway?" The vote was unanimous—guilty as charged. The jury returned to the courtroom, and Raoul didn't even blink when the foreman announced, "Guilty as charged." Roger was stunned. He was furious. His best friend had done him in! How could Raoul have voted guilty? Impossible!

But he had.

Roger took a deep breath, and before his lawyer could restrain him he jumped to his feet, waggled his fist at Raoul in the jury box, and yelled to the judge one of the better remarks ever made in the sanctified presence of the Maine Superior Court.

He shouted, "But—Your Honor! I'm the wrong son of a bitch—it's *him!*"

(Explanatory note: Asking the reason for this remark, the lawyer learned the truth, and the story came forth. Raoul said the testimony of the arresting officer was so convincing that he got carried away.)

Sweet Bells Jangled

B ack before one of our recent Christmases, a newspaper piece told about these people who don't want their children to sing Christmas carols in the public schools at Christmastime. The thought did cross my mind that Christmas is as good a time as any to sing Christmas carols, and that some people are awful hard to get along with. But my attention was diverted by the suggestion that "Jingle Bells" is all right for Christmas music—it's the naughty old ones like "Hark the Herald Angels" that are destroying the vital American way.

This threw me—a devout and persistent enemy of "Jingle Bells" at Christmastime—into a tizzy of confusion. How did "Jingle Bells" ever get accepted, even obliquely, as Christmas music? Sure, it's singable, and jolly, and real ho-ho-ho, but it's not a carol and never was—yet here it is about to be cited before the United States Supreme Court as the kind of Christmas music that doesn't offend people who are offended by Christmas music. (Perhaps you'd better read that again!)

The chap who wrote "Jingle Bells," name of Pierpont, lived in Medford, Massachusetts, suburban to Boston, and he didn't have a piano. It makes a story pretty nigh as good as that of the Austrian priest who did "Silent Night" in a snowstorm. In those days there was but one piano in all of Medford. Things are much better now, and I'm told Medford has three of them. But this Pierpont could set a note down on paper and sort of hear it with his eyes, so he didn't need a piano and he wrote "Jingle Bells." Then he took the sheet of music across town to a piano teacher who owned the piano, and he asked her to play it and see what she thought. He called it a "sleighing song," and he never had the slightest suspicion that it would become a Christmas carol preferable, to some people, to "O Holy Night."

Ah! Humankind might have learned valuable lessons in this respect as far back as the days of Herod the King, but nobody heeded, and we've gone along with persecutions and inquisitions, lopping off of heads of Charles the Firsts and baiting Quakers, hoorawing Cotton Mathers and nit-picking Christmas carols. The great religious freedom has been the right to shove your ideas down other peoples' throats. All on the "Jingle Bells" level. Makes me kind of proud that in my youth I was infused with understanding by the good Father Sean Skerry, who taught me the catechism. An unredeemable Black Protestant, I had a playmate who was the opposite, and every Saturday morning his mother would give him a nickel and he would go to the rectory of the Church of St. F. Xavier, where Father Skerry would "hear" his catechism lesson. My chum and I couldn't indulge in the frivolities of a no-school Saturday until after this lesson, so I would tag along and sit on a chair in the corner while Father Skerry officiated. Afterwards, my chum and I would go to the brook for a swim, to the beaver flowage for trout, to play scrub, to swipe apples, to pelt somebody's laundry, to fly kites, to pick blackberries, and to do any of the pleasures reserved for good Christian boys who are not encumbered by doctrinal differences and theological disputations. My playmate was a slow study, so by exposure I mastered his catechism long before he did, and I never handed Father Skerry a red cent. I used to repeat the catechism to my Jersey cow during the ceremony of lactation, and it soothed her. She also liked "Paul Revere's Ride" and "Young Lochinvar." It was to be years before I would wonder what Father Skerry would think of that, had he known. There is wisdom in tolerance and virtue in understanding. Cows are not spiritually selective.

The folly of differences was demonstrated by the two Free Will churches in our town of Orland. Orland is not a large place (eight hundred registered voters) and it seemed curious to many people that it would support two churches of the same persuasion, each across the street from the other. The answer was sheer jingle bells logic. Back along, there had been but one Free Will church, and the members had worshipped harmoniously. But there arose a difference of opinion, a schism in doctrine, a dispute, and a separation. Half the congregation had gone across the way and built a second Free Will church. It seems one faction believed that Balaam's ass turned and spoke to him like a man. The other group believed that Balaam *said* his ass turned and spoke to him like a man.

The acceptance of non-Christmas "Jingle Bells" as Christmas music suitable for non-Christmas programs at Christmastime reminds of the atheist community out in Oregon. In the early days of Oregon a group of atheists came and settled an atheist village. In the years that followed some Christians came to join them, and before long the population was about fifty-fifty. Then the little atheist children began to come home to ask their parents why they couldn't have a Sunday school. All the little Christian children went to Sunday school on Sunday mornings, and the atheist children didn't have any place to go.

So an atheist Sunday school was established.

How About Snoods?

Some kind of a Swedish research team with nothing better to do has announced that the chef's white cap is altogether too high. Snob symbols of cookery's caste system, the pileated billycocks range from the modest pretense of the humble fry cook to the lordly prominence of a full half meter for the executive busby of an Oscar. Kitchens have been built to accommodate these capotic high-rises and this, say the Swedish statisticators, is wasteful. Ventilation fans must be placed so high that efficiency is impossible, and valuable heat is exhuasted along with the effluvia of gastronomic philogistication. We're blowing dollars away. So we can be grateful that affairs in Sweden permit attention to such important matters, and once we put beanies on all the cooks we may again see Delmonico steaks at thirty-five cents.

The hat, in general, is ancient, but nothing from away back has been preserved for our inspection. From statuary we know that cooks did have an identifying tiara in early times, but seemingly it was not graduated in altitudes to identify abilities—it served all who wrought with victuals, chef to scullion. From the

hat he wore, you couldn't tell the stew man from the jelly roll. So we know the ancient kitchen was democratic and the haute cuisine was never in contention over plateaux of hauteur, so to speak. We don't know when the altitude of the bonnet began to distinguish skill and rank, but today the Cordon Bleu believes the *béchamel* boy should not beat the *béarnaise* in the *bain-marie*, and the height of the respective hats is important. *Nev-vaire* the twain shall beat! And this costs us *beaucoup* dough in lost energy.

To me there was always an element of pretense in the chef's

cap. Put one on anybody, and he looks like a chef. And, how would anybody ever become an acknowledged expert on *crépinettes d'agneau* if he's wearing a beany? Further, I knew a whale of a fine cook who never wore a hat in his kitchen, but because he disliked the feel of new dough he always kneaded his bread with his mittens on. He cooked at the Rappalonsis Lumber Camp for King Lacroix. I knew some other lumber camp cooks that would please the Swedish researchers. Such as Jerry Latouche, whose sartorial frippery at the range was a Kaybecker toque with a tassel in which he kept his money, his pipe and tobacco, his rosary, a deck of cards, and a photograph of his wife back in St. Prosper whose name was Harry. And Mike Borsak, who cooked in a "kossuth" that had gilt letters on the band saying, "I've been to Atlantic City." Mike had never been south of Bangor, and won the hat throwing baseballs on the midway at Northern Maine Fair. Neither Jerry nor Mike related headgear to cooking. They wore hats because their heads were bald as two eggs. Mike was the one everybody called Curly.

The Swedish research would like the snood. An interesting derivation. In the beginning a snood was a net worn by ladies to restrain the hair. When the hermetically sealed tin can was perfected for food processing, which came about here in Maine, women who worked in the factories were required to wear hairnets. Consumers disliked to find a stray wisp in the fish chowder or the applesauce. The "snood" thus became associated with food, and was a synonym for net. Along the Maine coast, the "twine" of fishing came to be called "snoodin'." A man who was stringy—lanky—might have the nickname Snood. And in the Maine lumber camps, any cook who wore a snood was sure to be called Snood, and sometimes Snoody. And what the Swedes need to know is that a kitchen staffed by snood-wearing cooks requires a very low ceiling, and has a high efficiency.

This is a good thing to know.

Some Personalities

At the end of the year, allowing two weeks for judgment, preparation, and scheduling, the TV brought us a review of the most important personalities. The show came on at 7:30 P.M., which is after my hibernal bedtime, so I didn't see it, but Bunny Bradstreet sat up for it and says none of my favorites was mentioned. Here are the important personalities of my year:

Hastings Littlefield of Outer Razor Island, who came to the mainland on December 23 to do his Christmas shopping. He keeps his automobile in Zeke Edgerley's barn, and as the battery was down he had to call Porter's Garage and it cost him $35.00 just to get started. Then he spent $878.95 in the Rockland stores, getting something for everybody, and came back to find his automobile had been tagged by the police for a traffic violation. The tag stuck behind his windshield wiper had places to check off fireplugs, crosswalks, restricted zones, overtime, and so on, and Hastings looked to see what it was he did wrong. The policeman had checked off, "Other," so Hastings went to the city office and paid $2.00.

Merton Munjoy, sixth-grade genius, who finally combined science and culture by programming the school's computer so it composed, "A Sonnet to the Gross National Product."

Gertrude Cimek, who was solicited to bake a cake for the annual benefit supper of the Ladies' Aid of the Community Volunteer Firemen's Association. She made a three-level vanilla cake with chocolate icing. Because it was snowing and she was home alone she then shoveled out the garage door and along the driveway

25

to the main road. Next, she drove seven miles to town and found a note tacked to the fire station door: "Due to Storm, Supper Cancelled."

Silsby Soames, who for seven straight months got a printout bill with compounded 18 percent interest penalty when he had paid the bill eight months ago. Having written seven letters, he wrote another.

Everett Malm, II, who keeps a lobster boat foghorn by his telephone shelf. He blows it vigorously into the mouthpiece whenever he is connected to somebody's leave-a-message tape machine.

Jackie Nesmith, who got an advertising letter from the Home Craft & Hobby Shoppe that started, "Dear Ms. Nesmith." He went into the store and tipped over a counter of loose buttons.

Gunther Laboute of the Meadow Road, East Shore, who was pushing a hive of bees on a wheelbarrow and absent-mindedly waved at some summer people.

Sissy Bomgard, who spent $38.75 for groceries at Benner's Market, and by mistake carried home the wrong bag. She has six pairs of used sneakers.

Luther Prindle of Cobb's Cove, also East Shore, who sent nine dollars for reregistration and stickers for his boat, learning too late that the old registration and stickers were good for two more years.

Dipsy Dunbar, townhouse custodian (janitor), who stood on the top step of a ten-step stepladder to replace a burnt out electric light bulb. He is resting comfortably at his home on Maple Avenue and can have visitors in the afternoons.

Shorty Connover, baseball statistician, who announced that Boomer Bagshot, left fielder for the Tri-Town Tigers, batted .218 against lefthanded pitchers and .218 against righthanded pitchers, for a combined season's average of .218.

Reginald Ransome of R.F.D. No. 3, Box 547, who saves all his junk mail and carries it once a month to dump on the postmaster's lawn.

Bruce Dunphy, letter-writing adict, who wrote a letter to the editor of the *Clarion-Bugle* to say the latest issue was excellent and he didn't find a thing in it to write a letter about.

Chet Ringrose, who drove 1,500 miles without finding a participating dealer in the big automobile pay-back sale.

Otis Oldheimer, spry and chipper at eighty-seven years, who

had his spirits crushed when a girl stood up in the bus and gave him her seat.

And Freddie and Clarice Sturtevant who, for their golden wedding anniversary, received not one, but two congratulatory messages from the White House.

Faulty Translation

The glad morning cry of a diligent and dedicated barnyard rooster is such a resoundingly joyous call that it seems impossible human beings could fight over it. But here it is, right in the newspaper—a couple of Germans in Bavaria are in court over the *kikiriki* of Tscheki. In Germany, it appears, roosters do not crow as they do here in the Boston States; they say *kikiriki*. True, those of us skilled in the languages know that when a German rooster stands tippy-toe on the Hühnerstange at Dämmerung and lets go with his *kikiriki*, it sounds very like he was saying cocky-doodle-do, but this is because of faulty translation. In France, roosters incline toward the tonic accent, and say *coquerico*, but this is close enough to *kikiriki* to be almost Teutonic. In classical Latin, the dawn cry of the bull chickabiddy was simply *galli cantus*, or song of the cock, and the name of the last military watch of the night derived from the rooster who sang at daybreak—the *gallus*—and was the *gallicinium*. This has nothing whatever to do with the cockyleeky of the Scottish highlands.

Which returns us to our story:

In the smallish commune of Landsberg, in Bavaria, lives a farmer, Hans Gebele, who has a now somehat famous rooster named Tscheki. Tscheki was not always Tscheki, but was just another scrub barnyard rooster until he was taken into court as a common nuisance, and a reporter on the Landsberg *Blatt* thought a rooster in the news should have a proper name. Tscheki is, therefore, a *nom-de-plumage*. A neighbor of good Farmer Gebele, and consequently a neighbor of Tscheki, one Rudolf Kofron, complained that when Tscheki went *kikiriki* at dawn's early light it roused him from the rest to which he is constitutionally entitled, and thus Tscheki should be rendered null and void in the public interest. I have no information as to why the judge decided as he did, any more than I have any notion of why our judges in the United States say foolish things, but the beak in Landsberg agreed with Plaintiff Kofron and Tscheki was remanded to the stewpot. Bauer Gebele has appealed, and Tscheki is on his personal recognizance—biding with his pertelotes and kikiriking as has been his wont. In his appeal, Bauer Gebele has asked the court to take notice that said Kofron once put up a spite fence, indicating that he is hard to get along with, and that "a person of more or less normal sensitivity will find the crowing of a rooster a thoroughly enjoyable thing." There is also a contention that if Neighbor Kofron has constitutional rights, so does Tscheki, and a suggestion, which I think is a dandy idea, that Neighbor Kofron move to the city.

The town in which I grew up was on the main line of the railroad, and had fifteen grade crossings within the village limits. An engineer was required to blow two longs and two shorts on the locomotive's steam chime whistle for each crossing. Just about midnight, seven times a week, the Boston to Halifax "Maritime Express" would roar through town at a sustained speed of 80 mph. The compact part of town, where the fifteen crossings lay, amounted to about a mile and a half. If you want to put your slide rule to this, you'll find that the engineer on the Halifax train blew sixty times in a bit more than one minute. We were a rootin-tootin town.

But, the Halifax train usually ran in two sections. The first, making fewer stops, had the returning fish cars and the sleepers. The second had the work cars, mail and baggage, and the coaches.

Allowing five or six miles as a safety distance between sections, this meant that four-five-six minutes after the first section passed, the second section would arrive—with another required sixty blasts from the chime whistle.

Relative to Tscheki and his *kikiriki,* the people in our town thought this midnight hullabaloo was a natural consequence of affairs, and instead of pestering a judge about it, we just got used to the noise and lived with it. An interesting thing is that some nights, for want of passengers or fish cars, the Halifax train would run in just one section. This would pass through town with the usual sixty blasts, and then in four-five-six minutes there would follow an unaccustomed silence that woke everybody up.

I commend the moral of this parable to the justice of the Bavarian appellate court who is considering the fate of Tscheki. Perhaps he should ask Kofron to move to Munich. Perhaps he should just tell Kofron to learn to like Tscheki. Because even Kofron is going to be unhappy if we ever come to that dark morning when the world has no chanticleer to rouse the orient sun.

Except the Eggs

This story is just as true as any you'll ever hear out of the State of Maine. Seems our good friend Nathaniel Bowditch Sinnett, only year-round resident of Outer Dovetrap Rock— *rock* being a Maine coastal euphemism for an island—got a codhook through the ham of his jigging hand whilst pursuing a haddock chowder in its native lair, and finding it bothered him some he ran up the flag on his fishhouse. Marty "Gundalow"

Bascombe, across the way on Tinsnip Island, saw the flag and rowed over in his dory to find out what it meant. He decided Natty needed better attention than he could give him, so he cranked up the motor in Natty's boat and ran into Smeltrun Cove, where there's an old folks' home. The nurse there fixed Natty right up, and he's all right, but the codhook was a total loss. It was now something like half past two, going on three o'clock, in the morning, so Natty and Marty decided to wait for daylight before going back down the bay. They took some sleep in one of the vacant rooms up on the third floor, and breakfasttime they sat down with the fifteen-twenty-odd old folks and tucked away some food.

While they were eating, an "interviewer" arrived from the State Department of Humane, Ecological, and Helpful Services for Gracious Living, Bureau of Statistical Investigation, and she began asking questions about the general situation at the Smeltrun Cove Old Folks' Home. Not knowing that Natty and Marty were what you might call transients, she asked them the questions, too, and they told her they thought everything was finest kind, except for the scrambled eggs. After breakfast, Marty ran Natty back to Outer Dovetrap, rowed his dory back to Tinsnip, and the two of them went separate ways about their affairs—said affairs being seaward and remote.

Now, the food service at the Smeltrun Cove Old Folks' Home is a contract job handled by a catering firm in Schenectady, New York, with a regional manager in Sanford, Maine, and an area distribution center in Bangor. The result is "institutional food," but this company services a number of schools, hospitals, and so on in Maine and is proud of its long record of dietary and gustatory excellence, and to put things in focus, it takes its scrambled eggs very seriously. So when the service manager was notified by the State Department of Gracious Living that there had been a complaint about the food at the Smeltrun Cove facility, the computers went to work and the next day there was consternation in the home office at Schenectady, New York. Immediately, further details were asked for, and along the chain of command this request came at last to the resident house mother at Smeltrun Cove—this was the first she knew about any complaint. She knew none of her happy old folks had complained and presumed the whole thing was a mistake until she happened to recall that Natty and Marty had freeloaded a breakfast, so she wondered if the complaint might have been something of their doing. She knew both boys from away back, and they would never be malicious—could this have been their idea of a joke? Anyway, there was no need of a tumult, so she notified the catering command that there was no need to pursue the matter.

But the catering company wanted its good name untarnished, and didn't want the State House on its back, so it asked the interviewer of the Humane Etc. for more specific information. She, feeling this challenged her position, got uppity, and in snotty mood replied that the complaints had been made by Mr. Nathaniel Bowditch Sinnett and by Mr. Martin Bungalow (sic) Bascombe, at breakfast, such and such a date, and the item complained about was scrambled eggs.

So files were pulled, sources of fresh eggs located, telephone calls made, and everything in the long line of ordering, receiving, forwarding, opening, cooking, and serving scrambled eggs seemed in order. The catering firm decided the interviewer was either misinformed or was trying to start something. Things were sticky enough so a trouble-shooter was sent to find Natty and Marty.

He hired a lobsterman at South Overlook to run him down the bay in his boat, and when he found Marty and Natty he asked them just what was the matter with those scrambled eggs. He brought back their complaint: "Not enough of them."

Two-Horse *Lalage*

In this great age of speed and dispatch, when a war that will kill millions will last only three seconds, there should be some recognition of the two-horse citizen. Composed and relaxed, I don't care if school keeps or not.

Here at Back River, "boat people" are the summer mahogany folks who come to Maine "from away," in full possession of our nonpublic access, to scare the cats, disturb the dogs, raise a dust, and perform the yachtsman's routine of readying the boat for those glad weekends ahead when it will be too foggy to sail. The boatyard by our shore (hauling, storage, repairs, brokerage at owner's risk) isn't too bad a neighbor. As I watch the boat people who support it I can see that their keeping a boat is much more of a job than I make. I keep a boat, but it doesn't consume me, and I find plenty of time for my philosophies and philanthropies. *Lalage* does not intrude as other boats seem to, and I haul her myself and save money.

I built *Lalage* one winter from select white pine and firm red oak, taking my time. I named her classically for the ladylove of Flaccus in Liber I, XXII. She is fourteen feet long and is powered by two ash oars, with auxiliary equipment of a two-horse *horsbord*. In Maine coastal terms she is a skiff, flat-bottomed, seaworthy, tight as a cup, and trim. The Latin I carved on her stern sheets is meant to perplex these boat people who say port when they mean left, abaft the aft when they mean astern. My seamanship is the pure Bellman kind, with rudder afoul the bow-

33

sprit, and the garboard off the binnacle. But I did know about Lalage, and my stern sheets read:

DULCE RIDENTEM LALAGEN AMABO

Even though I look off on the Atlantic Ocean, *Lalage* has never been in salt water. She was built for a special purpose: once a year she is taken from my boathouse (which is also a woodshed and catchall) and rides in my pickup truck to Caucomogomac Lake to engage in the togue fisheries for a week and ferry Bill and me on our picnics. Togue is Maine for a lake trout, and Caucomogomac is pronounced cock-m'gommick. For two decades Bill and I have devoted the middle week of each July to this

indolence, and we conduct our Maine wilderness pleasures in
low-key dignity. Buying the two-horse outboard motor for *Lalage* established us as oddballs in the era of hustle. This is the jet
age, and nobody should dawdle. I went to three dealers in marine
matters and got essentially the same response: "A two-horse
motor! Aw, come on—you don't want anything like that! Here,
look at this beauty!"

They thought Bill and I should push sweet ladylike *Lalage* up
the lake with one of these fifty-horse jobs that wash out loons'
nests. With the first dealer I tried to explain that we wanted a
two-horse for *Lalage* because she goes too fast when I row, but
he continued to pat the fifty-horse giant and to insist that he
knew more about what I wanted than I did. With the next two
fifty-horse pushers, I didn't try to explain—I just walked out.
Then I found a fine old gentleman of moderate habits who handles used things like trundle beds and stereoscopes, and he
understood. He had just the motor for *Lalage*, and for me and
Bill. Two-horse, and just exactly the motor—one day Bill and I
started back to camp after a picnic, heading into a light breeze,
and after churning *Lalage* for a half hour we were a mile behind
where we started. It's impossible to explain the satisfaction of
that to our local boat people. It made me think of Dr. Hahn, and
while I rowed to give the two-horse some help I told Bill about
Dr. Hahn.

Dr. Hahn was a physician and surgeon from Massachusetts,
and he owned an "original" Friendship sloop named *Depression*.
She was the oldest Friendship sloop afloat; he had bought her
for little or nothing back in the Roosevelt days. He faithfully
brought her each summer to the homecoming regatta of the
Friendship Sloop Society here in Friendship harbor, and as
faithfully competed in the races down Muscongus Bay. Year after
year, every race, *Depression* came in last. I saw the doctor on the
street one afternoon and asked him how he made out in that
day's race, and he said, "Fine! I got two pails of mackerel!" The
doctor's attitude toward speed always appealed to me. I liked to
watch all the other sloops straining every effort to win trophies,

with *Depression* limping along behind with the mackerel jigs astern. With lines out, Dr. Hahn was always my special winner.

On my lathe, I made rollers so I can move *Lalage* by myself. I have a hoist that puts her up into the pickup and lets her down again. Simple devices demonstrated, back when Lalage was a little girl, by Archimedes. I pay no boatyard fees. In ten minutes I have *Lalage* ready to go, and another ten minutes unload her at the lake. A classic little lady who requires no more than that is worthy of respect, and Bill and I appreciate what we have. We sit up and ride in what Bill calls "deliberate speed," and *Lalage* moves with stately dignity, in Asclepiadean serenity, making us, we feel, unusual in today's larruping love of celerity.

Now and then Bill looks up from his fly-rod handle to say, "Molle atque facetum."

Wrong Piece!

Something happened right here, and it made me think of Bill Nye. Nobody has thought of Bill Nye all these long years. What happened is that I had a piece right here that I used once before in another book, and as I read the thing over before mailing the stuff to the publisher it sounded familiar. So—Bill Nye. Let us consider Bill Nye for a minute, because he was worth it. Bill had several books published in his time, and each was a different color. Red, green, blue, and so on—and he said this was so the readers could tell them apart. Bill Nye did repeat himself some, and it didn't bother him that the same piece was in several books.

Speaking of Bill Nye, the three granddaughters came for a weekend, and paused on the way to attend a performance of

Annie at the summer playhouse. They liked it, and arrived all a-sing. Grumpa dulled their enthusiasms by asking them about the songs, and did they know anything about this Annie? Something gave me an inkling they didn't. Which was so. They told me all about the vacant-eyed youngster in the prolonged newspaper strip, about a dog named Sandy, and about Daddy Warbucks. Being a dedicated student of all the letters to the editors about what's wrong with our public schools, I related, and as for Annie—what are our schools supposed to teach, anyway? How come three bright girls, all good readers, can attend one of our better school systems, get better than average grades, and yet their doddering old grandfather has to tell them about Little Orphant Annie! How does a school system delete James Whitcomb Riley from the inculcation of our cultural heritage? So I recited:

An'all us other children, when the supper things is done,
We set around the kitchen fire an' has the mostest fun
A-list'nin' to the witch-tales 'at Annie tells about,
An' the Gobble-uns 'at gits you
   Ef you
     Don't
       Watch
         Out!

Then I told them to go to the library.

I also told them to look up Bill Nye, too. I know that Bill Nye's connection with Maine is tenuous, but he was born in our town of Shirley and that fact might lend local color to their literary research. Bill Nye and James Whitcomb Riley teamed up on the lecture circuit and worked together a good deal. Riley would come on stage and repeat his *Little Orphant Annie* and *The Raggedy Man* to give the audience some Hoosier sentimentality, and then Nye would follow with what amounts to preposterous Down East humor. He'd tell about the boy who stuck his finger in the molasses syruptitiously, about how he spoke to a felloe *(sic)* in The Hub, and about how every rich man in America was once a poor boy except Dr. Mary Walker. One critic was amazed that Nye came on stage, peered as if in a poor light at the audience, and then spent several minutes wiping his spectacles. The audience went into gales of laughter at this, and the critic couldn't understand how wiping eyeglasses could be funny.

Born Edgar Wilson Nye at Shirley in 1850, he left Maine as an infant to go to Wisconsin, and later to Wyoming. At Laramie he founded his newspaper, *The Boomerang*, and his writings were widely copied, bringing him more fame than money. His letter to the postmaster general acceping the postmastership at Laramie was soon followed by his first book of essays, and that in turn by his equally funny letter to Queen Victoria, in which he discussed royalties. In the meantime Riley, who was one year older than Nye, had gained a similar fame from his writings in the Indianapolis *Journal*, and their several joint tours across the country packed all halls along the way. When Bill Nye moved to the New York *World* he gained a bigger readership, and ". . . as Bill Nye says . . ." became common in American conversations. His *History of the United States* is an American classic, if forgotten. For one thing, it had the magnificent cartooning of the great F. Opper.

Bill Nye had some lecture segments that were not all that complimentary to his native state, and there were some Mainers who took offense. He told how a boy would bug potatoes all day and then take his girl for a sleigh ride at night, and he had several similar comments on Maine weather, customs, and geography. So the story goes that one day a selectman of the town of Shirley was in New York, and he called at the *World* office to speak to Nye. He told Nye that a sign had just been attached to the house in Shirley where Nye was born. Pleased, Nye asked what the sign said, and the selectman told him it said "Greenville—Six Miles." That compensated for the cracks about Maine.

Oh, yes—I now have three granddaughters who know that Little Orphant Annie is not really a "comic" strip. And that Edgar Wilson Nye became "Bill" Nye when Bret Harte wrote his *Plain Talk from Truthful James*. That's right!

Abed and David

O ne of my Brice Booker stories ("How to Buy Wood," from
Twelve Grindstones) suffered the profitless indignity of
going into an anthology of Maine literature, but I think that was
not my best Brice Booker story. Descended from shipbuilding
and seafaring traders, the three Booker boys were old Brunswick—Bill had a lumberyard, Emery was a banker, and Brice
was a sharp trader who dealt in anything and always seemed to
be running to catch up, as youngest brothers often must do. He
was, as the yarn in the anthology tells, the wood buyer for the
U.S. Gypsum Company, something which hardly interfered with
whatever else he might find to do. He auctioneered, did some
surveying, was an appraiser, and opportunity never knocked
but what he heard. He was shrewd and needed to be watched,
but his basic principles were honest and he never lied unless he
had to. Bill and Emery were just a couple of Bookers; I preferred
Brice and had many happy times with him while he enriched
my background with anecdotes and folklore I could refinish and
sell. So I think my favorite Brice Booker story has to do with the
time he locked horns with Will Jordan and came off second best.

In their time, it was said that my grandfather and Horace Jordan each made a living trading off the other. It was somewhat
so, and as one would stick the other, the other would contrive
to stick back, and they went through life outwitting each other
with cows, manure spreaders, woodlots, and whatever else made
a good chance. Horace had a saying that was strictly his; it was
like a trademark. It was, "Bigod you, Mister!" He'd say, "Lovely

mornin', Bigod you, Mister!" Now this Will Jordan was the son of old Bigod-you-Mister Horace, and in his turn he, too, had a saying. He'd say, "Aye-yes, that's the story of Abed and David."

The "aye-yes" is probably a State o' Maine development that came from the early Scots. Accustomed to saying aye, they would add yes in deference to the English and Irish neighbors, and (my guess) this came over into Maine coastal speech as our unique eyah. So Will Jordan took on the ancient aye-yes and added the story of Abed and David, whoever they were. He used it to mean that's the way the ball bounces, the cookie crumbles; equivalent to the Frenchman's "Ca va!" In the surrounding ten townships, make a remark about Abed and David, and everybody thought of Will Jordan. Now, in the early 1930s Will Jordan operated a portable sawmill on a lot near Allen's Range Road in Freeport, and after he'd stripped the lot he moved the mill along, as was the defoliating custom of portable sawmill people of that day. A few days later in the First National Bank of Brunswick, Will was approached by Brice Booker, who made some overtures that didn't fool Will Jordan one bit.

Then Brice said, "See you've moved the mill."

"Aye-yes, that's the story," said Will.

"Looks-if you left some good stuff in the yard. You going to clean it up?"

"Depends. What did you have in mind?"

"Well, I got a truck and a couple of boys, and I could set them to cleaning it up—must be a few boards and dimension stuff there worth looking at."

"Aye-yes," said Will. "Might be." Will now knew that Brice was about to make an offer. "I ain't looked around to see, have you?"

"Not really, but they's always some scoots and scantlings— I'd be doing you a favor. How about ten dollars?"

"Aye-yes," said Will. " 'Twould save me the trouble, but I wouldn't want you to lose money on it. See what you get, and ten dollars sounds about right."

Brice told me about this long afterwards. He said he put the boys on the lot, and they got one good load of two by twice, several loads of fair boards, a lot of edgings, and all the heavy timbers out of the saw carriage foundation. Brice said his brother Bill took all the edgings and sold them in his lumberyard for kindling wood, and that alone took care of his agreement with Will Jordan. Then he saw Will again in the First National Bank.

"Mornin', Will," said Brice. "How-ya doing?"

"Just gittin' by," said Will.

Brice said, "Here's ten dollars for letting me clean up that lot."

Will feigned not to see any ten dollars, looking right over the money at Brice. "What did you find?" he asked.

"Some pretty good stuff."

"Much?"

"About ten truckloads, some better than others."

"Aye-yes," said Will. "That's the story. Ten loads. Let me see—ten loads at ten dollars a load. That's an even hundred."

Before Brice could say anything, Will went on, "Aye-yes. I distinctly remember our handshake. Ten dollars a load."

Brice told me, "I gave him the hundred. I made enough so I was well ahead. But can you imagine anybody pulling a swindle like that? And didn't that bahstid go and die right after that! Never gave me a chance to get even."

"Aye-yes," I said.

And Brice said, "That's the story of Abed and David."

Leaping Lobsters!

An Italian named F. Marvan has written a book called *Legends of the Sea,* and I have been wondering about him. The book is translated into English by David Macrea, is pub-

lished by Crown, and is printed in Italy—a gratuitous disclosure all literate nations will applaud, since in Italy typographical errors seem to run about five pecks to the bushel. Our local library bought the book thinking it would interest our three hundred-odd lobster catchers (some odder than others) but so far this seacoast village has shown little interest. The color pictures in the book of the ocean in many moods are delightful, but after a few pages of text the tide seems to ebb. Well, I guess that the author did not fare forth to look upon the ocean in its grandeur, but did his research in a library. Page after page runs to quotations from Homer to the goddess of the Norwegian sardine pack, and the legends are strange to ponder. Fairies come from seaside grottos to steal sheep, and things like that. Early on we are told that classical writers knew nothing about the tide, as the Mediterranean has no significant ebb and flow, and then follow remarks about the tide by Pindar, Aristotle, Menander, Herodotus, Epictetus, Alcibiades, and more. And I insist the tide does not bound. Even with a bore, it doesn't bound. I gave up on the page where it says in Asturias the fisherfolk say that when lobsters leap it is a prediction of foul weather. I should think as much. How pleasant to see a lobster burst into the air from the depths!

Here in Maine where we know a good bit about lobsters and the sea which nurtures them, a leaping lobster is never regarded as a prediction at all. He's just a comical cuss who got carried away in some submarine exuberance. The Maine word that goes with lobsters is "crawl." Lobsters do swim, but not in the Maine dictionary. When you ask a Maine lobsterman if he had a fair catch, you will say, "Were they crawlin'?" He will respond, "Daow!"—this is an emphatic negative, but since no Maine lobsterman ever admitted he made a penny, it means he did very well. Then, if you open the subject, he will tell you that no lobster ever leaped. But a Maine salmon will leap, and if you see one leap it means the ice has gone out.

There are no Maine legends of the sea in that book. The purpose of Mr. F. Marvan, I think, was to be erudite and profound, whereas the true Maine legends of the sea run to the amusing. His legends are grim and dour. Haunted by the souls of drowned men who come to weep there, the casuarinas trees of Tahiti (Marvan says) "talk at night." That's not very good for a real bang-up legend. The Maine version, just as good but far more entertaining, has the talking trees on Rack Island holding a speaking contest every Friday afternoon. Odd that Marvan has nothing in his book about the Fundy tides—highest in the world.

Nice little legend about them. When Paul Bunyan was a baby, down at Machiasport, his large size made it imprudent to cradle him in the house. One lurch in his sleep and he'd knock down a wall. So his daddy and his mummy made a Moses cradle, boat-style, and moored him offshore every evening at beddy-bye. One night the tyke was restless and he turned and tossed some, and the waves he set up swamped fifteen British warships anchored down the bay. Those waves have never subsided, and account for the tremendous tides in the Bay of Fundy.

The Marvan book does considerable with mermaids, but the

mermaids of Hancock Point are not included. These come up from the ocean once a year when the August moon is full, and they go into Lon Libby's field and pick blueberries. Lon caught one in a purse seine one year and kept her in a rain barrel until Blue Hill fair, when he exhibited her in a tent.

Another story about the Hancock Point mermaids was told by Archie Macomber. Said he was hauling traps one day and he thought he saw one of these mermaids swimming by, a fathom or two under water. Thinking he'd like to have one, he jumped overboard and tackled her. Turned out it wasn't a mermaid at all, but a porpoise, and there was Arch hanging on for dear life with a porpoise he didn't really want all that much. A porpoise swims with an up-and-down motion, not like a fish, and Archie said this made it very hard for him to keep his hat on, but he headed the thing for the beach and finally got ashore. The Coast Guard brought in his boat the next day.

We have a wonderful legend of the sea right here in Muscongus Bay that would have done a good deal to pep up that Italian book. Has to do with Chief Norumbee of the Micmacs, who was spearing hake off the ledge on Muskrat Island one day, and his moccasin slipped and the poor joker went into the drink. Swallowed right up; last was ever seen of him. But if you go out to Muskrat Island at high water and stand on that ledge and stamp your foot and shout, "Chief! What are you doing down there?"— Chief Norumbee will answer, nothing.

Up in a Sling

W hen the president of the United Auto Workers got his name in the papers by saying the Japanese automakers should be required to build factories and make their product in the United States, Kendall Tweedie said, "Oh boy! Ain't they got their arse in a sling, though!" This colorful, if indelicate, metaphor is easily explained. What Kendall meant is that by its own foolishness the United States auto industry has brought upon itself a certain just retribution, with the overtone that it has nobody to blame but itself. Kendall was thinking of the old days on the farm when an ox would be taken to the farrier to be shod.

The horse is better adjusted than the steer, and can stand on three legs. The blacksmith can lift one hoof at a time and fit shoes to a horse, but if he tries to pick up one hoof of an ox, the foolish thing will fall down. Shoes could be fitted to an ox in a recumbent posture, but that would be unhandy for the farrier and was never the answer. The ox sling was a kind of gantry, and a bellyband operated by a small winch picked the beast off the floor and suspended him for a fitting.

The ox is cloven-hoofed, and the shoe for each foot comes in two pieces, so it takes at least twice as long to fit an ox than a horse. So for twice the horse-time an ox would hang there in innocuous desuetude, placid and helpless, while the smith went around him. There is nothing more helpless, and little that looks so comical and stupid. And the ox has brought it on himself—there would be none of this indignity if he'd learn to stand on three legs.

If, perchance, there *is* anything more stupid and more comical, it is a horse in a sling, and that happened, too. Blacksmiths had ways to persuade reluctant horses, some of them downright, but when a nag came along that needed one, the ox sling was waiting and up he'd go. No credit to him, because he was a horse and could stand if he'd a mind to. His predicament, like that of the auto workers, was ridiculous. Thus slung, horses had a tendency to kick and squeal—oxen were less rambunctious—which just made things worse. Farriers, in extreme instances, would just let the cussid ding-ding hang there until he cooled down. Up in the lumbering country, where there was an urgency to keeping a horse at work, blacksmiths often saved time by slinging a horse that might have been cajoled in another way. One reason, I suppose, for less slinging in the villages was the great clamor of a slung horse, and the concomitant vituperation of the blacksmith. But in town or in the woods, the ox sling was almost always used on the "green" horses from the West.

Nobody has ever explained to me why all the horse people were mad at the State of Maine. For a hundred years, no Western horse ever arrived here that was kind and courteous. If the West did, now and then, manage to produce a decent horse, great care was taken to send him someplace besides Maine. The green horse was a wild animal that had been rounded up and driven into a boxcar, and he'd get off the train here in Maine mad at everything and looking for trouble. Now and then a farmer would need a new horse, and would dicker and haggle, but in the woods the green horse came in bunches and had a season. Lumber was harvested on snow, so lumber camp horses put in the summertime lolling about at a "farm." In this sense, farm has a special meaning. It was a place to grow hay, a pasturage, and a base or "depot" camp for a timberland area. Pittston Farm, Grant Farm, Michaud Farm—the names persist but the need for the old-time "farm" has passed. So, in the fall a crew would make a lumber camp ready for winter, and the horses would be brought from the farms and stabled in the "hovel." It was always necessary to replace some, and along with whatever veterans came through the summer in good shape would be enough green horses to make the total. And, the very first thing that had to be done with a green horse was to shoe him. The opening week or so of a camp was always called "starvation days," because the cook hadn't organized things, but that opening week was also hard on the ears, as the blacksmith slung green horse after green horse and the things chimed throughout the forest.

I speak from personal knowledge, and I understood exactly what Kendall Tweedy meant about the United Auto Workers. I had a boyhood brush with a green horse. Gramp had picked her up because she was cheap and because he needed to start haying. He was an old hand at "breaking" a horse, and would do that soon enough—but first she had to go to Craig's blacksmith shop. Somehow he got a halter on the creature, with a rope, and then he threw a blanket over tractable old Tanty so I could sit up horseback and lead the new cyclone to town. She followed Tanty along all right, and I had no trouble. But Jim Craig, the smith, decided he didn't want his shop kicked apart and he slung her. She kicked and squealed and everybody came to see. Jim tied a rope to each of her legs and had two-three men hold on each, and from across the street I could look in the big door and see him working.

And Salted Down

This is a good time to eulogize Richard M. Dorson, who died in Bloomington, Indiana, on September 11, 1981. I owe him something. Dr. Dorson was professor of history at Indiana University, and an authority—perhaps *the* authority—on American folklore. As a pioneer in this fertile field he ticked me off on folklore *(The Jonesport Raffle)* and amused me for years as he sought the Mother Lode and elevated my bread and butter to new depths of academic culture. He could take an ancient Down East doozie that State-o'-Mainers keep on tap for the summer complaints and bring it off on the equal of *Hamlet* and *Paradise Lost,* winning additional grants to make further study. Dr. Dorson was editor of the *Journal of American Folklore* and swiped quite a few of my yarns.

In pursuit of this topic, our own University of Maine at Orono (that's Or-no) took up folklore, and as something of a tribute just about the time Dr. Dorson was laid to rest brought out a handbook on Maine folklore. Our professors researched well, and then fed the "get" into a memory bank. Get? The get is what folklorish fishermen call the catch. I hope—I plead—that somebody in this hurtling world is sensitive about putting folklore into a memory bank. Anyway, a button was pushed and the computer wrote a book about Maine folklore. The impropriety of this seems not to have offended anybody except me, although perhaps Dr. Dorson's trailblazing conditioned people so they are no longer sensitive.

There is an elusiveness to folklore—the manners, customs,

and legends of a people. It is not something that can be clapped in a can and salted down. It should never get electronic scrutiny, or be "stored." Folklore floats along calmly and gently with the tide, pleasantly keeping its own place until some busybody picks it up rudely to look at it. Psychology teaches that when you analyze an emotion you lose the emotion, and when a Dr. Dorson "studies" folklore it fades, dissolves, and there he stands with his Ph.D. askew. The Midwest university professors who flock to Maine every summer on government grants to collect our folklore do not know this very well, and easily become the victims of our jolly old folklore characters who have been practicing their eyah's all winter. They don't realize that when you break out a tape recorder and ask a Mainer to talk Down East, he ceases to be himself and becomes a Clark Gable. "Eyah," he says, "Finest kind!" And he playacts with the contrived material meant to entertain folks "from away." Each Labor Day these professors go home with another ninety-and-nine versions of:

"Where does this road go?"
"No place—stays right where we built it."

Or:

"Lived here all your life?"
"Not yet."

I assure everybody with no academic nuances whatever that it is possible to live in Maine without hearing anything like that in the usual flow of normal living, Mainer to Mainer. But you let a professor show up with a clipboard, and he'll get all the variations from the first ten Mainers he "researches." This explains how the folklore evidence mounts with every sabbatical that Maine folklore runs 185 percent to saucy rejoinders to tourists—which pleases the tourists. "Think it'll rain?" "Always has." (Or, "Be a long dry spell if it don't.")

These professors never take into account that all Maine folklore has two sides. It depends on who tells it. An example: Years ago Wash Libby was haulin' traps out by Halfway Rock, maybe fifteen miles at sea, and he sees a stinkpot summer-mahogany job coming, clip-topping the swells, and Wash is some horn-swoggled when the bo't fetches up, swings alongside, and speaks him. Wash assumes (which turns out to be correct) that he's caught some Marblehead jokers kiting down to Baw Hawbor for the weekend. "My good man," says a cockytoo in a yacht bonnet, "might we purchase some lobsters?"

All right. There's the situation, and there's going to be a big splash of Down East folklore.

Wash had found them crawlin' that morning and he was guessing at three kentals for the gang, maybe more, so if this fancy wants lobsters, Wash has 'em. With folklore.

"Boy lobsters or girl lobsters?" says Wash.

"Does it make a difference?"

"That depends," says Wash.

"Depends on what?"

"Depends on what you're going to do with them."

"How so?"

"Boilin', boys; but for a stew, no."

"We plan to have them boiled."

"Boys it is, then," says Wash, and, "how many?"

Do you see? This folklore is going to depend, in its turn, on whether you hear about it from Wash or from the stinkpot people.

Wash told me that when it came to paying, he didn't have any scales aboard, so he guessed at the weight. But price didn't matter, and the man just said, "How much?"

"Well," said Wash, "they's one-fifteen a pound in at the Cove, but away out here like this I'd have to get one-thirty."

When Wash was telling me about this, he said, "Well, what was I to do? They was expecting me to make like Maine, so I felt obliged to make like Maine and give 'em so'thin' to quote and laugh about, and that's easy worth fifteen cents a pound. Maybe if I'd-a took more time, I could-a got 'em up to a dollar and a half."

Dr. Dorson, could be, might like to wait around and see what a computer memory bank will do with a thing like that, but I'll move along to something else.

Two Housekeepers

A gentleman in his eighties who is distant kin to me and a widower of several years writes that his housekeeper is retiring and he hopes to find her replacement. He says his hopes are not high—he would like to find an agreeable woman in her fifties who drives a car (if she hasn't one, he will provide one), bakes bread, won't raid his raspberries, will go easy on the lobster, and can play a slide trombone (secondo) by ear. The reason he tells me all this is not with any hope that I can find him such a housekeeper; instead, he wanted me to know that in this enlightened day and age the newspaper wouldn't print his advertisement.

The girl behind the classified counter made him cross out everything that might be discriminatory (age, color, sex, tempo) so that when the notice appeared he got an application (amongst others) from a man thirty-one years old who said he'd like to try housekeeping and see if he liked it. My kin was shaken by this when the man telephoned, and said he would have to think things over. My kin was not impressed by a male with that ambition, even if presumptive, and like most Mainers will continue to think of housekeeping in the feminine.

This set me to thinking that I've known two housekeepers—not counting my bride who bakes bread but can't blow a trombone. I just barely remember the first, who was Lizzy Jordan. She was a vast woman who was otherwise prominent because of a cleft palate and a hare lip—difficulties now covered by "speech impediment." Only those who had known Lizzy a long time could understand a word she said, and my grandfather, who employed her, had not known her quite long enough so much of the household routine was snagged in faulty communication. After Grandfather was gone and our old farmhouse had burned, Lizzy married, but she was single in my memory and the only instrument she played was the Edison phonograph.

As a boy, coddled and mothered by Lizzy whenever I visited Gramps, I was not so much awed by her as curious. I never really got accustomed to her, and this was too bad because she took good care of Gramps in his need. She was a good woman. Her cream-tartar biscuits were so light they needed a plate over them to hold them on the table, and she knew how to build a custard pie up to four inches, sill to ridgepole. Lizzy, had I understood what she was saying in those times, was uncouth, a fault of fetchin' up, and it was well my tender ears didn't appreciate her when she would bawl at Gramps to take off his muddy barnyard boots before he set foot into *her* kitchen. The Billingsgate fishwives would have conceded. So let's just say I had plenty of reason to remember Lizzy Jordan.

Aunt Hapsy was nothing at all like Lizzy Jordan. Aunt Hapsy, my mother's sister, is the second housekeeper who came to my notice. She, too, was unmarried and played no instrument. But when I heard that Aunt Hapsy was a housekeeper, Lizzy came to mind, and I was in for a big surprise. She was not to be hefty, she spoke quietly, and her diction was perfect. My mother, holding my small hand, made a call on Aunt Hapsy one afternoon, and we applied at the rear entrance of a considerable mansion in Boston's suburban Brookline. A young lady in apron and cap led us up some stairs and into an office room with a huge bay window. Aunt Hapsy, trim, was behind a big desk dictating to a secretary. She waved the secretary away to rise and greet us in family fashion and she hugged me as a loving aunt should. I remember my ear pressed something cool on her bosom, and when she released me I saw the beautiful gold watch pinned to her shirt with a fleur-de-lis. I saw her lace collar, too. Aunt Hapsy was as far away from Lizzy Jordan as could be. Aunt Hapsy was an *executive* housekeeper, managing a ménage with fourteen servants and a full program of social events. The ownership of S. S. Pierce considered Aunt Hapsy a very important customer.

Aunt Hapsy retired to her native Canada and lived briefly into her second century, still unmarried. On her hundredth birthday she received the traditional congratulatory cablegram from The Queen. Aunt Hapsy, loyalist all the way, was delighted thereby, and this has amused me because to me Aunt Hapsy was always much more regal than Her Majesty. I guess maybe Lizzy Jordan was, too.

She Starts,—She Moves,— She Seems to Feel the Thrill of Life Along Her Keel . . .

E verybody should go to a launch and thrill, too, as a new hull gently, imperceptibly at first, starts down the ways, gaining until, as Poet Longfellow precisely says, she "leaps into the ocean's arms." If they don't have launches today wherever you are, it's well worth the trip to Maine, where now and then we do. Longfellow knew what he was writing about, as witness his rhyme of "stanch" with "launch." If you come to Maine for a launch, you must learn to say lanch—it's the Maine way and Maine was ever the place for lanches. The first craft lofted and lanched in the New World was the pinnace *Virginia*, 1607 at

Popham. At that time the name Virginia was really a localism, and what we now call New England was then North Virginia. Popham is just across the bay from Friendship, and this whole area has been splashing boats into the tide ever since. The other day we all went to see the latest, the *Leeman*, slide out of the ramshackle Lash Boat Shop into Hatchet Cove. She's not the prettiest thing the Lashes ever built, but beauty is not essential to work boats. The *Leeman* is a sturdy and stanch dragger, meant for the deep sea fisheries. Now that she's overboard, she'll be fitted with heavy masts and great winches (that's *wenches*, you know) to handle the gear for the Deep Ground. She's a fisherman.

The Lashes have lanched a great many work boats over the years, a good many of them being the sloop. Back in 1622 when the Pilgrims came from Plymouth to look Maine over, fancying themselves quite alone in a New World, Governor Winslow put in his journal that he was astonished at the great number of sloops flitting about the islands of "the main." That same summer 132 English vessels took on fish caught mostly by those sloops, and until the perfection of the gasoline marine engine the sloop was the Mainer's work boat. Loveliest in style was the Friendship sloop, developed here on Muscongus Bay for local purposes. Gaff rigged, the Friendship could be handled by one man, the fish hold was ample, and her lines were equal to the rugged seas she would meet. The basic sloop developed later into the Down East schooners—the Marblehead, the chebacco, the dogbody, the pinkie, the filebottom, and also whalers like the Tancook. The Lash Boat Shop built many Friendship sloops, every one of wood, but the more recent ones have been for recreational sailors. They'll make you one.

Winnie and Son Wesley operate the shop now. Some say their sloops respond to spoken orders, like a well-trained horse or dog, and they "sail themselves." Saying their boat shop is "ramshackle" is not a slur—master boat craftsmen need not be house carpenters, and so long as the shop shelters the hull there is no need for style. Summer artists pass up the Lash Boat Shop as too improbable to paint. This new *Leeman* has a high house, so the boat shop roof was adjusted and a plastic bubble raised. Now that the *Leeman* is lanched, the bubble may or may not be removed. We can only wait and see. "Been that way ever since I can remember," an elderly lobsterman told me, "but you don't come to a lanch to look at the boat shop."

When the *Leeman* was freed, she daintily, for all her heft, rode down the ways to be cheered in the usual way. When snubbed, she stood high astern, because her ballast and her derricks had not been added. How does a craftsman with a lead pencil and a board to write on lay down a boat so she'll ride true when, after launching and after finishing, she is ready for sea? I must ask Win Lash some day, not that I need to know, but that I expect his answer will be worth hearing.

The lanch of the *Leeman* was a very small event compared to lanches in the bygone days of sail. When the *John A. Briggs* was lanched at Freeport, in September of 1878, seven thousand people attended, including Governor Alonzo Garcelon and presidential candidate James A. Garfield. Most came by their own means, but the Maine Central Railroad ran special excursion trains, and the island steamers brought folks by water. The launching banquet, a festive luncheon that included beverages as stanch as the *John A. Briggs,* gave Candidate Garfield a chance to politick, but 'twas said the folks were not in a mood for that, and he cut himself short. The lanch of the *John A. Briggs* was about average for those days.

But the lanch of the *Leeman* had a good crowd, considering. After she was afloat she got the usual visits and inspections, and according to ancient usage Win and his workmen were already laying the keel for another boat. This was good news, because nowadays orders for wooden boats are far apart, and so are lanches. Which is good reason not to miss one if you get a chance. No—Winnie Lash does not spread a traditional lanch banquet for a modern-day boat like the *Leeman.* But you'll be glad to know that here in Friendship a lanch is still good for a school holiday. As we started home after the *Leeman* was tied up, we met the village schoolteachers leading their youngsters down over the banking to the beach. There would be a lanch banquet after all. Each youngster had a picnic basket.

Gross Lots Only

He was persistent as an Ontario mosquito, and it took me a good half hour to get rid of him. Perhaps that makes him a good salesman, but he irritated me until curiosity took over and I wondered why he called on me anyway. His "line" was the little giftie the businessman gives to his customers—calendars, thermometers, conversion tables, pens and pencils, pocket diaries. This was my first brush with enticements for the GNP, and while we all know the aggressive merchant gets his thingamajigs somewhere, I never knew that a salesman called and waded right in. He shook my hand so my cap flopped up and down, and indicated he had been waiting for this pleasure for thirty-five years. I was certainly fortunate that now we were in touch and he was at my side to bend every effort. My business, he said, would improve and increase as we dealt together in unity. How many calendars did I think I could use?

Then I understood. This joker was the latest victim of my several signs, and in all innocence had hoist me on one of them. The last laugh would, as usual, be mine, but I didn't have it yet and now I would be obliged to say *no* to all of his proffered business stimulaters, only one of which interested me. That was a ball-point that wrote in five different colors, but not all at once. Everybody has long accepted this man's wares from hardware stores and insurance agents—yardsticks, pocket calendars—but not everybody has seen the complete line in the man's sample cases. I succeeded in kicking him out before he got halfway through.

My home workshop is my temple of dalliance. I putter and I whittle and I scrimshaw, and some days I do nothing. The nearest I ever came to crass commercialization was the time Pouty Pontier came in to have me bore a shearpin hole in his haulin' shiv. Took but a minute, but it saved Pouty a trip of fifty miles to a machine shop. Pouty said, "How much?" and hauled out his wallet. I laughed, and to pass the matter off and maintain my amateur standing I said, "Bring me a short lobster some day." Pouty never brought me one. And now this supersalesman of enticers and stimulaters was telling me how to double my income.

I've gone to great trouble over the years to avoid such. Everybody likes to come around and suggest things for me to do, and wants to interrupt my sitting around. I know that I can make five whirligigs about as fast as I can make one, but then I'd have nothing to do for four more times. If I decided to make four more, that is. My philosophy is specialized. The assembly line is not for me. "Tooling up" offends my sensitive niceties. I have been working on a digital steeple clock now for quite some time. I think a digital steeple clock doesn't need to be finished to engender the chuckles of kindred spirits. The original steeple clock sat on a shelf and the pendulum could be seen wagging through a glass door. A digital clock has no pendulum. So, why a steeple? Good question. I suspect five hundred ball-point pens that write in five colors, but not all at once, are not likely to augment the sales of digital steeple clocks. I do not want to labor in an urgency that forces me to complete my steeple clock while there is yet time. But this salesman heard me not, or wouldn't, and after five or six no's I asked him what made him think I wanted any of this junk?

Every business, large or small, he told me, needs the warmth of pleasant customer relations. A small gift, now and then, helps. "What business is this?" I asked.

I have several signs, and I didn't know which had caught his eye. He pointed at the one which says:

SHIP CHANDLER
Since 1708

It isn't much fun to have to explain a thing like that. As I tried, he looked at my workbench, my tablesaw, my lathe, my planer, and also at my digital steeple clock. He began packing up his samples, and he said, "Then, just what *do* you do?"

Brought to mind the Do-Do store, upstate. The two Michaud brothers carried on an old family store, and became vexed at the outrageous claims of an aggressive competitor across the street who was using newer methods. He'd offer Sunny Monday soap at ten bars for a quarter when he didn't have a cake of Sunny Monday in the place. He'd tell customers he was sold out, and then they'd come into the Michaud store and want to know why they couldn't get Sunny Monday ten for a quarter. So the Michaud brothers bought the only newspaper advertisement of their lives, and it came out a full page and it said:

> *We Don't Say We Do Much,*
> *But What We Say We Do—*
> *We DO DO!*

Difference with me is that what I say I do, I don't. This trinket salesman didn't believe me and wagging his head he walked off. He was looking at another sign:

> *Notice to Customers!*
> *Commencing July 1st*
> *Bakers Peels in Gross*
> *Lots Only*

And so maybe I got the last laugh.

Passive Periphrastic

There's a strong loyalty towards Latin by those who have looked into it, but otherwise it goes unendorsed. But I am agreeably surprised that a few faithful linger, and whenever I reveal that I know a genitive from an ablative they like to write and commend me. Not long ago I mentioned my high school toga, as the garb of our Latin Club, and it was amazing to hear from all the old fogeys that 'fessed up to wearing togas. Expecting no such response is hardly complimentary to our public schools, where Latin has been a naughty word for lo. For those who share my thoughts, I have a reward:

Some scholars have long surmised that the ten lost tribes of Israel moved on until they became the North American Indians. Some don't. I believe the testimony of Moroni supports this presumption. And I have discovered, and now reveal, that on their way those lost tribes paused long enough in Rome to gain some smattering of classical Latin, as I shall now explain:

Here in Maine we have a public television channel which originates a quiz show called, "So You Think You Know Maine?" Four contestants line up and a quizmaster asks them questions about Maine geography, history, institutions, personalities. One week came the question, "Write down the Maine county names that derive from the Indian." That's not much of a question. Maine has but sixteen counties, and the three oldest use English shire names—York, Lincoln, Cumberland. Washington, Hancock, and Franklin came from American heroes. As to the Indian names, there would be Androscoggin, Penobscot, Sagadahoc, and probably Aroostook. And when the four contestants on that TV show held up their cards, to prove that they did know Maine, all four of them had included Piscataquis!

But that's not all! The quizmaster looked at the four cards and said, "Correct!" And with my old high school Latin toga in mind I sighed for the lost tribes of Israel, and turned off the TV so my wife and I could play cribbage.

While we're at it, the new importance of old-time firewood might encourage the study of Latin, which did give us Piscataquis, if rightly applied. We were four children, and I was the first to discover the right time and the best place to do my Latin homework. There was always the evening session, but I found it helpful to rise early and run over my Latin one more time. In the depth of winter this meant coming down from a cold bedroom before daylight, into a kitchen that was relatively warm where the banked-up wood fire had dozed the night in the range. Behind our kitchen range was the copper hot water tank, which kept warm, and by it the chest of drawers in which Mother kept towels and other kitchen gear. So I would come down to kick open the front damper of the range, shove in some wood, and climb up to perch on the chest of drawers with my back comfy against the hot water tank. By the time I had run through my Latin assignment the kitchen would be toasty and Mother would appear to begin breaking eggs. I used that perch, and so did my brother and two sisters, and we parsed and passed. Which is a good kind of thing to have in your memory. It teaches that with a good wood fire a child may be comfortable and learn Latin at the same time. Nothing like a good copper hot water tank to help along the conjugations.

There was one bad morning. My younger sister, in her turn, came down to the kitchen, opened the damper, put in some wood, took the perch, and snuggled against the tank. Vercingetorix was getting it for fair when the hot water tank reacted. It had been a very cold night and the dozing wood fire had not kept the water pipes from "catching." As the fire roused, steam built up in the copper tank, and while my sister reclined and

declined, a Vesuvius was hatching and making ready to aston-
ish her. She was fortunate not to be blown through the roof
when it went off. She managed to escape into the dining room
ahead of the burst of steam, unhurt.

My sister then cranked the old magneto telephone, and when
Gladys Mitchell, the operator, said "Number please!" my sister
yelled, "Gimme a plumber!"

Gladys wanted to know, "Which one?" Is it not good to know
that in a two-plumber town we had a high school that offered
four years of Latin? Gladys might have rung Fred Taylor, who
sang in the Baptist choir, but she didn't—she rang Wildcat Smith,
who did not but who was the chief of the fire department, and
when Wildcat responded my sister shouted, "Our buster's
boilted!"

Wildcat immediately recognized that as a muted synecdochi-
cal accusative, and he came right away with a new buster.

Patriotic Peas

It's a shame, really, that the rest of the United States doesn't
realize what Maine and Massachusetts do for Patriot's Day.
Otherwise unnoticed, Patriot's Day goes back to 1775 when Maine
was part of Massachusetts and Paul Revere rode to alarm the
embattled farmers. It is the 19th of April and the anniversary of
the Battle of Concord and Lexington, known in Lexington as the
Battle of Lexington and Concord. In Massachusetts, to observe
the occasion, Sunday soldiers in Minuteman uniforms do colorful reenactments, and Paul Revere always rides again. He is
played, these days, by a zealous member of the Hibernian Horse
Marines who has drunk a good breakfast, and there is some

confusion with St. Paddy's Day, which is also Evacuation Day and something like Patriot's Day only different. The impersonated Paul generally contrives to fall off his horse now and again, and for the past ten straight years he has galloped through Medford Square, where he is supposed to stop for ceremonies, to a series of ineffectual whoas. Nothing of this sort happens in Maine, where Patriot's Day is not now much of a patriotic occasion, although last year a summercater from Worcester showed up with red, white, and blue hotcaps for his tomato plants.

Maine's observance centers around green peas. Green peas are traditional for the Fourth of July, and the 19th of April, Patriot's Day, is the last clear chance to plant and crop. It is astounding that the planners of our Revolution foresaw this, and arranged two holidays to meet the requirements of the seed catalogs. We resident Mainers try to get our first row of green peas into the ground as soon as possible after the frost leaves, and do not wait for Patriot's Day as such. It's the seasonal visitor who comes up from Massachusetts just because it's a holiday there to see how his cottage wintered, to take off the battens and turn on the water, and to plant his peas. This has become ritualistic, and after he has done the Patriot's Day chores he will return to Massachusetts and we won't see him again until the next holiday, which is Memorial Day. The summer season is about to set in and while he may commute, his wife and children will come at school-out to stay until Labor Day.

We have one part-time neighbor who actually comes from Lexington, and the derring-do of the Redcoats means nothing to him. He hurries up the turnpike, and the minute he arrives here he telephones all around to say, "I'm home!" This proves life is valid only here on the nonresident tax list, and time spent in Massachusetts is wasted. "Welcome home!" we return. Then he takes off the blinds, opens the windows as aforesaid, and gets the picnic chairs and tables out on the porch so he can get to his tiller. He needs to go to the store for fertilizer, and if he favors the telephone peas he must set stakes and wire. As the sun sets on Patriot's Day in Maine the thing you hear is not a shot around the world, but the summer complaint bragging that his peas are in. One man who cultivates a small crevice between ledges out on an island always brags that he planted twenty-three rows, but his rows are only two feet long. He comes from Hingham.

Peas properly planted on Patriot's Day will do all right. Our cold and wet Mays don't hold them back, and when the man comes back for Memorial Day it's soon enough to hoe them. We Mainers hoe sooner, but we're here. Both of us come out about even, and Patriot's Day planting will provide a July Fourth mess. So the rest of the country ought to take up Patriot's Day the way we do. It makes our Fourth of July a real pea-picking holiday.

Natural Ingredients

Things in this mail order catalog are said to contain "only natural ingredients." The hucksters have been around long enough so I am not beguiled into thinking this means anything in particular, but I found myself balancing it off against other items that "contain no artificial ingredients." Maybe I have done what the people who make catalogs have never done—gone to the dictionary to look up *ingredient*.

Dominique LaPierre was one of the finest cooks ever to ply his trade in a Maine lumber camp, and his name is still legend along the West Branch of the Penobscot. He would give the recipe for his real-honest-to-gosh Kaybecker pea soup to anybody who asked for it—except that he always skipped his "secret ingredient." Dominique, whom we called "Minick," did make a dandy, and if you don't use the true Quebec yellow split peas and *beaucoup lard* it won't be pea soup at all. Anybody knows that, except the people who can pea soup. Minick would start his pea soup about the third week in August, when the cruisers came in to lay out the choppers' winter operation, and the huge pot remained on the back of his cookshack mogul until spring. The contents would go up and down with a tide suited to the lumber business, as Minick added and subtracted on a continuing basis. The old imparted flavor to the new. On some days the soup was less rigid and on some days a spoon would stand up in it, but the nutritional power remained about the same and Minick was much loved. At ice-out in the spring, Minick would hoist his pot of pea soup onto the wangan wagon, and he followed the drive, feeding four square a day all the way to the mill. Then Minick would have the bullcook scour and grease his pea soup pot, and he would go home to San' Lazare in Quebec to comfort his *bonne femme* Rozee until August came again.

Now, Minick's "secret ingredient" was nothing but pond water. Pond is pronounced pound—Chain of Ponds is *shine-a-pound*. And most pond water in Maine is potable—or it was in the long-log days up-country. So h'every morn-NING Minick would send his little cookee down to the "pound" to fetch two pails of wattaire for the pea soup. Spring water and well water just wouldn't suit. In the winter the cookee would have to chop ice to get pond water, and Minick believed the little pieces of ice made a difference. His mixture *(mixture* being no more than a combination of *ingredients)* was too popular to question this belief, so Minick always insisted on pond water, and *voila!*

So, and talk about ingredients! One day the cookee came back, and he had a chunk of ice with a big fish frozen in it. Wan dem t'ings you call heem *wananish*, but we Mainers know it as a salmon. Minick hove the ice, fish and all, into his pea soup pot— and *there* was a triumph! They still talk about that pea soup all up and down the Penobscot River. Finest pea soup Dominique LaPierre ever made! Tasted just like fish chow-daire.

It occurs to me that you probably cannot find a more natural ingredient than pond water, and I can't feel that a salmon would be artificial. The health food people would probably object to Minick's mixture. But I can see him now, whenever somebody asked him how he made his pea soup. He would lay a finger by his nose in the best manner of the Cordon Bleu, and he would enumerate. Five hundredweight split peas, two hogsheads salt pork, and so on. You could go right home and start a batch. But he never said pond water—just water. That's why nobody ever made so fine a pea soup as Dominique LaPierre.

Around the World

When Mother bell advertised that operators would announce their names—"Good morning, this is Nancy. May I help you?"—I resurrected a truism that I'd uttered years ago: That the telephone company is run by a bunch of people who don't know how to run a telephone company. The new way, the advertising said, will make telephone service more personal. Gracious! Back when Myrt and Gladys sat at the switchboard, telephone service *was* personal, and friendly, and in many ways more reliable and useful. But Mother Bell's minions scrapped all that and forced the impersonal upon us until telephone service needed just one thing to bring it back to sense—personalities. Permit me to relate about the time I wanted to telephone around the world.

Mother Bell scheduled a series of advertisements that said, "Now you can talk around the world!" Thinking of Magellan and the good press he got for the small time he put in, I decided I'd like to be the first person to talk around the world, so when the first advertisement appeared I dialed the operator at once. We had toll centers then; I don't know where mine was, but the girl offered to help, except that her tone of voice was neither Myrt nor Gladys. She was impersonal as a sheet of plywood. "Yes," I said. "now, let's take this slowly. I'm on an unusual

tack, and I anticipate resistance. I beg your indulgence, and hope
you'll bear with me."

"Is this an emergency call?" she asked.

"Not yet."

So I told her I saw in the magazine that I could now talk around
the world and the idea intrigued me. I said, "I can't very well
talk around the world to myself, so I'd like you to ring my neighbor across the way, Jim Tucker—he's home now and I can see
him through his window." Fact is, I could see his telephone on
the wall right by his elbow. Be amusing, I thought, to see him
jump when the bell rang, and reach for the thing, and then see
his reaction when I told him we were talking around the world.
So I gave the toll operator his number.

She said, "But that's a local call! You can dial that yourself."

"You haven't been paying attention," I told her. "I want this
call to go around the world."

The silence was total, and extensive. "Hello, hello!" I said.
She said, "I'll let you talk to the supervisor."

The supervisor indulged me, and seemed to grasp what I had
in mind, but she was baffled. She did say, "Oh, I understand
. . ." with a rising inflection that meant, "Boy, oh boy! Have I
ever got a ding-dong now!" But she honestly gave me the right
answer. She said, "I'm frank to tell you, I wouldn't know how
to set that call up."

"Well, Frank," I said, "somebody somewhere must know how
to set it up, or this advertisement wouldn't be in the magazine.
Why don't you go to work on the idea and call me back?"

"That's not my name," she said, and when I asked her what
her name was she wouldn't tell me. "It's against regulations,"
she said. And the next afternoon I had a call from a manperson
who said he was the traffic superintendent, and could he be of
service? I told him of my burning desire, again looking across
the way at my neighbor's telephone. "Yes," he said, "that's the
way I heard it." I got the idea my burning desire had been well
discussed in telephone management circles, and he had been
instructed to talk me out of whatever it was I wanted. This he
began to do.

Well, I never did make that call. The man from traffic ran out of prepared remarks shortly, and reverted to a manner that I must admit was personal. He told me right out that some countries that would be relaying such a call were not technically ready to do so, and that fear of failure made him leery. He certainly conveyed his own belief that the call would not come off, and then he said, "Besides, those ads mean you can now talk anywhere in the world—we never meant 'around' the world."

So I said, and I thought with some reason, that maybe Mother Bell should change the wording of her advertising.

And, do you know, in a couple of weeks the wording in those advertisements was changed, and I read, "Now you can call anyplace in the world!"

And a personalized voice will say, "Hello, this is Barbara . . ."

Speed-Letters

Any Suggestions about how to handle these cussid speed-letters?" asked Neighbor Nate out of the blue. Me, if some company writes a speed-letter to me, I cross it off my list and take my trade across the street. They're uncouth, rude, discourteous, and irritating. You know what I mean—these ready-made forms with carbon paper, so when you use one you have a copy for yourself, one for the addressee, one for the town library, one for filing with IRS, one for the school board, one for instance, one to make ready, and all for one and one for all. Oh, yes—and one for the other chap to use for his reply. The speed-letter is supposed to be the busy man's friend, but if the joker doesn't care enough about me to use a decent letterhead and compose a polite letter, that's that. I told Nate I pay no attention to the things.

"Well," said Nate, "the one I got, I think you might do something with it. Didn't you hear the fire engines last night?" This is Nate's story:

Said he was talking to Larry Hedstrom last March, and Larry said he had found the best stuff for cleaning chimneys. "Chimbleys," he said. Larry had been to Nova Scotia, and he picked the stuff up in a store there. Digby, he seemed to think. Little plastic container with a blue powder in it, sort of, and it said to lay a spoonful on the embers of a fire, either in a stove or a fireplace, and—puffo! All clean all the way up the flue. Larry said he tried it when he got home, and it was just the greatest. Took a mirror and looked up his chimbley, and it shone like a bottle. Beats anything else I ever hear'n tell of, he said.

So Nate asked him what it was called and he couldn't remember, but when he got home and found the little plastic container he telephoned to Nate with the address. Said it was called Floo-Scoot and it was put out by the Mukluk Chemical Works, Limited, in Coreopsis, Nova Scotia. (Names of places and people have been changed to protect the guilty). So Nate ups and writes to the Mukluk Chemical Works, Limited, in Coreopsis, Nova Scotia, and he tells them he would like to buy a supply of their Scoo-Floot, or whatever it is, and where can he find it in the Boston States? Nate told me he had a very dirty chimbley at the time and he was hoping for a quick reply, but it was three weeks before he got a good letter expressing pleasure at his interest in their product, and telling him it was distributed in the United States by the Wigwam Distributing Corporation of Walpeeko, Michigan, and Wigwam would be in touch shortly.

Nate said about that time the spring broke up and he put in a row of peas and painted the shed. The garden came along, although he got some late blight on his Early Rose potatoes, and then he got the haying done a good week ahead of common. Didn't feel the need of a fire as the summer wore along, but he still had that dirty chimney on his mind because it sure did need cleaning and it probably would fire off with the first coolish evening. Then Nate picked his factory beans and got the wood under cover. And come September there was a coolish evening, and

he touched off a few kindlings and his chimbley caught. I didn't
hear the fire engines, but Nate said things were nip and tuck for
an hour or so. Then Nate says, "So in this morning's mail, I gets
this cussid speed-letter from the Wigwam people, and they tell
me Floo-Scott can be had from Brigham's Hardware Store down
in Springfield, Massachusetts."

Not a Cane

Piece in the paper explains that walking sticks are coming
back, and that a walking stick is not a cane. That is true,
and my Uncle Bert learned that from my grandfather. When Uncle
Bert married my Aunt Grace, they settled in at housekeeping,
and my grandfather shortly went to visit them to look over his
new son-in-law. He got a neighbor to come and feed the stock
and pick up the eggs, and took the steamcars. Uncle Bert and
Aunt Grace met him at the dee-poe with the Maxwell, and after
supper Uncle Bert suggested they take a stroll and see the neighborhood. As they stepped out the door, Uncle Bert reached a
cane from the umbrella stand and handed it to Gramps.

Gramps never used a cane, but he well knew about walking
sticks. He flourished this one a couple of times to get the hang,
and then noticed Bert didn't have a stick. "Where's your'n?" he
asked.

Bert said the wrong thing. He said, "Oh, I don't need one."
That instantly changed the walking stick into a cane. Grandfather, older, was doddering and infirm; Bert was the bride-
groom rejoicing as a strong man. "No more do I!" said Gramps
as he tossed the thing behind him on the piazza, and off he went
to walk rings around poor Bert.

Some years after Bert's mistake (the cane, not the marriage), I came along, and Gramps walked the legs off me, too. We'd start from the house to go up the lane, over the knoll and down into the woods, and his stride was altogether too much for my little legs. As I grew taller, he grew older, but age never shortened his gait and I was always behind. He was a small man, and one day I was taller than he. He still outwalked me. You see, he was a comrade of the old G.A.R., and when soldiers were moved in our Civil War, they were marched. Little Gramps, then with his mere eighteen years, struck out in the rhythm of the regiment, hay-foot-straw-foot down the map, clocking off the miles to Gettysburg and on into The Wilderness. The only people I ever knew to keep pace with my grandfather were his fellow comrades of the Sixteenth Maine Regiment of Volunteers, and every Decoration Day they would hike to the cemeteries with their little pots of geraniums at a clip that kept the band in quick time.

Had Uncle Bert carried a stick that day, Gramps would have without question, because when he walked about his farm he always had a stick. But never a cane. As a starter, there was always his peeled willow wand, his persuader for the cattle in the pasture lane. It stood by the tie-up door at night, and was left at the pasture bars every morning to be retrieved in the evening for the return to the barn. This stick was worn jauntily, with all the grace of a British swagger stick, and it could never be construed as a cane because the other end never touched the ground. A light touch or a smart rap, as needed, kept the cows moving along the lane.

Another kind of cattle persuader was by the tie-up door—the goadsticks left over from the days of oxen. Mainers called the goadstick a gad. There was some use of the gads as walking sticks in my time, but in the days of oxen a teamster always went about with gad in hand, whether teaming or not. Uncle Niah's gad had a murderous-looking darning needle in its business end—some three inches long. Uncle Niah had been gone for years, but Gramps explained to me that the needle was for show. Uncle Niah was, Gramps said, a nash old poop who blushed if somebody said darn, and so kindhearted he wouldn't slap houseflies. His animals were trained to whispered commands, and he'd plow all day and never touch his gad to a beast. (By the way—who first translated Martin Luther so he says it makes a difference whose ox is *gored*—didn't he mean *goaded?*) There was another old goadstick in the tie-up—instead of a brad it had a short leather thong to be used as a stinger. Somebody back along preferred to whip rather than brad. And then there were some plain sticks there—two or three of them I peeled in my time.

My first one was a hazel shoot, with a crooked root making a handle. Gramps and I, going with the cows, had stopped at the Red Astrachan apple tree to estimate the time to the first pie, and I jumped at a limb to grab down an apple to make the test. Gramps, with his cow stick, simply tipped one off the twig and caught it as it fell. "You need a stick," he said, and out came his "toad-stabber." He lopped off the shoot, and later I peeled it. That was the day he told me about the time Uncle Bert thought he was an old man.

Hawks and Handsaws

When I was but a tyke, Uncle Levi, our family's dearest kin, was making little Louise a doll's house, and he needed a few small items of hardware which could then be had from the Woolworth's of the day, the five-and-dime. Uncle Levi was a brickmason by trade, but liked to putter at what he called the "joiner's bench," and he was craftsman enough to make some lovely things. So, needing some hardware, he came down off the scaffolding where he had been laying bricks, riding in the mortar elevator, and he walked over to a Woolworth store to select his needs. He found them on a counter, and holding them in his hand he looked about for a clerk to take his money. There was no clerk. He walked up and down the aisles, called out "Hello, hello!" and came back to stand around and wait. Still no clerk. And as his noon lunchtime was nearly over he simply walked out of the store without paying and became a shoplifter. He told us about this when he came home that evening, showing no regrets for his depraved action, and said it served old man Woolworth right for not attending to his business.

The doll's house was weekend work, so he didn't get to putter with it until Sunday, when he found the hardware he had stolen didn't suit. It was too big or too small, or something, and he was greatly put out at his own stupidity for picking the wrong things. He put the hardware in his pocket and took it to the construction job the next day. Come noon hour, he again descended in the mortar lift, walked over to Woolworth's, and returned the several items to their compartments and slots on the counter. He then looked around and found just the right things that he should have had in the first place, and again tried to find a clerk to take his money. No clerk. So again he walked out without paying, to become the only shoplifter on record who exchanged his merchandise. The doll's house, by the way, is extant.

As I grew along, I spent much time at the joiner's bench with Uncle Levi, and he broke me in to the use of hand tools and the shaping of wood into pretty things. About that time the town meeting embraced manual training and domestic science in the schools, after long urging by the alleged educators, and Uncle Levi advised me to enroll for manual training. I did, but soon withdrew. In our town of shipwrights, the manual training shop came to be ridiculed as the Necktie Rack Works, and professional woodworkers who still believed in apprenticeships soon saw the folly of trying to make culture out of a craft. Uncle Levi understood when I told him the teacher had held up a handsaw and said, "Now, boys, this is a handsaw." It happened that Willy

Beakers, whose father made sloops, stood beside me in that class, and Willy had quite a business going as a saw filer. It occupied him after school, and he'd rush home to file saws until supper time. He got twenty-five cents a saw, and was considered the best filer in miles. Willy didn't stick to manual training any longer than I did, but we both made a necktie rack before we quit. Willy pulled out entirely, but I stayed on and "took up" mechanical drawing to finish out the term.

Uncle Levi was dismayed. He was afraid I was about to become an "arkiteck" and he hated architects. At the news, he went behind the barn and sat on the chopping block to "catch a breath." When he returned, he lectured me on the evils of architecture, and I have heeded ever since the great lesson he taught. He held a brick up under my nose, and he said, "All right, now, boy—this here ain't no handsaw, it's a brick!"

Having thus established a big difference between knowledge and what is taught in school, he clapped his bench ruler to the brick and read off its dimensions—length, breadth, thickness.

"Now, Johnny-boy, if you're going to draw designs on a trestleboard, don't you never forget them figgers! Every damn' arkiteck in this world should jump out of bed every morning and yell them figgers out the window to prove he ain't forgot 'em! But, I'm telling you once and for all—they ain't an arkiteck in Christendom that knows how big a brick is!" I never saw Uncle Levi so worked up, 'fore or after.

What boiled him was simple enough. All the years that he had been laying bricks, one after another in the interminable courses of the construction trade, he had to follow blueprints laid down by architects who didn't know the dimensions of a brick. Every time he had to leave a hole for a window of a door, the architect would specify dimensions the ordinary brick couldn't meet. Instead of six bricks, or twenty-four bricks, the hole would take five and a half bricks, or twenty-three and a quarter bricks. The brickmason had to break bricks to come out even, which slowed the work and added to building costs. Uncle Levi hated to break bricks. So I learned that this would be a far finer world if we never had an architect in the family. Shoplifters, yes—but architects, no.

(Seven and three-quarters times three and three-quarters times two.)

No Haulin' Day

A couple of old-time schools of "communications" recently gave up, pleading lack of funds, and I thought at the time that communication comes in different sizes. With new electronic opportunities, ordinary schools of "journalism" became schools of "communications," and the ability to enunciate a one-minute commercial for brass polish took on academic stature. All to the good, but when a school of communications can't communicate its need for money, a small doubt about something or other should be permitted. Not too many have been privileged to see some Maine lobstermen communicating without saying a word, partly for want of an invitation to attend, and partly because lobstermen get up about 2 A.M. to do their communicating. I think a school of communications is unlikely to work this into a seminar.

There are esoterics. The Maine lobsterman is a loner by nature and rather much by trade. Even when he "goes two," which means he has a stern man, or assistant, the arrangement goes "snacks" and neither is the boss. The Internal Revenue Service, back along, tried to tell the Maine lobsterman that going snacks, share and share alike, had to be handled taxwise as employer and employed, causing a tidal hilarity that bounced along the Maine coast all one summer. Much of the satisfaction of being a lobster catcher, I'm sure, derives from being out there in your boat, man against the sea, having every bit of the beauty and the challenge for your very own. Few lobstermen admire to have a rider, a visitor, and while almost every summercater would love to "go to haul" to see what it's like, invitations to do so are seldom. As a retired highlander coming to live by the tide, I was much touched when Harold asked me if I'd care to go haul "some mornin'." Some foolish people might prefer a seat on the Supreme Court bench—I went to haul.

But at his independent best, the Maine lobsterman stays close to all other lobstermen. While hauling, his eyes keep attention over the water to see who's around. If a motor fails, and some boat isn't back in harbor on schedule, community uneasiness settles over the waterfront, and you could cut it with a knife. Those who have "come in" recollect where they last sighted the boat—off Mosquito Rock, down east'ard of Rack Island—and there is a kinship framed in anxiety. Minds are turning as to where to look first. Then, when the overdue boat returns to harbor the tension eases, nobody admits to being concerned, and all go home to supper. The communion is reserved for members only. That first morning, when I arrived in the pitch dark of 2 A.M., Harold spoke a casual greeting and wanted to know if I was "down for the summer." Just to remind me that I was a guest; that I was different. Harold was standing shoulder to shoulder with Tom and John, and some others were there I didn't know or didn't recognize in the dark. "Mornin'," I said, and got silence. Everybody was communicating, and I joined the witan to face the harbor and wait for light enough to see the lobster boats on mooring. Fueled and with bait aboard, the boats would not cast off and go down the bay until the big decision had been arrived at as to whether or not this was a "haulin' day."

To haul, or not to haul?

Was this a day to run five, six, seven miles to sea, to be there at sunup when the law permits traps to be lifted, and would the sunrise be propitious? Nobody spoke, and the silence was communication.

After a time, Harold said, "Well—I dunno."

Some minutes later, Tom said, "Well—I dunno."

There began to be some light, and the shapes of the fishing boats appeared. Another few minutes, and John pushed his skiff off the wharf into the water, stepped in, and quietly skulled off toward his mooring. So, too, did Tom, and the others, and so did Harold and I—Harold taking the thwart to row his overloaded skiff. A decision had been made and agreement arrived at, and the day was a haulin' day. We were well down to Magee Island when the sun burst from the ocean and dripped great red blobs back into the tide. John, when he pushed off his skiff, had said it would be like that, but not in words. He just communicated.

On the other hand . . . A year or so later Harold stopped by and I gave him some Brussels sprouts from my garden, and I asked, "They crawlin'?"

"Eyah," said Harold. "Some."

"I haven't been to haul this year," I said.

Harold smiled. "You can go anytime you want, you know that."

"Eyah."

He looked at the Brussels sprouts and said, "That's enough. I'm good for just about that many once a year. They don't taste so good second time."

"You haulin' tomorrow?"

"Plan to."

" 'Bout four?"

"Prolly. Four-thirty, more likely."

I said, "If I'm not there by four-thirty, I'm not coming."

I was there at four-thirty.

On a haulin' day, Friendship harbor comes to life all over. Each engine, some three hundred of them, is started and idled long enough to listen to the rhythm. It must sound right. Pumps empty the bilges. Each lobsterman gets his waterproof clothes, because no matter how calm the weather, water flies when the pot warps are brought in over the snatch-blocks. The cumulative roar of all the engines keeps up until the fleet disperses "down below." Radios are turned on, and talk will continue among boats until the business of hauling warps interrupts. Friendship is a working harbor, and the fishermen have little use for the summer mahogany. Even if they did, one can't start up a motorboat and head for sea without making a noise, and once the fleet is outside Garrison Island the cottagers and the yachtsmen can go back to sleep.

Again, I found Harold, with Tom and John and the others, standing in the dark facing the harbor—communicatively silent. I got the usual small hello, and I got the foolishness about being down for the summer. I had my breakfast and lunch in a clam hod, weather gear under my arm, and as a touch of light developed in the east I could see that Harold's skiff (incidentally, one I made for him) was on the wharf and hadn't been bailed after last evening's shower. There was no surge of engines off on the harbor. I didn't hear the squawk of a boat radio, turning to the Coast Guard weather. Nobody said, "I dunno." Nobody had gone off to mooring. They knew. A decision had been reached and it was unanimous. John went first, shuffling up the ramp in his rubber boots, and then one by one they all went home.

It was not to be a haulin' day.

The First Day

There is no culture west
of Framingham.—Henry Beston

Now and then I get letters, always from west of Framingham, asking me what I meant by such-and-such. Such as "good." The questions arise from my devotion to the solecisms of my beloved Maine, and I must explain first off that good is always pronounced in two syllables—goo-ood. Numerous Maine words do the same—stow-wer for store, show-wer for shore, hee-yer for hear and here, and shoo-wer for sure. Of the many Maine ways to use goo-ood, I prefer the meaning of the French, "ça suffit." When Harold the lobster catcher comes to sup with us, the moment arrives when he is asked to replenish his supply.

"Harold," says my wife-person, "how about another chop?"

"No, no!" says Harold, "I'm goo-ood!"

This is the simple equation. The compound equation is used, for example, when she asks if he'll take more pie. "No," he says, "I'm goo-ood," and thinking that might be construed as uncomplimentary to the pie, he adds, "But that pie is some goo-ood!" This is almost the supreme Maine approval. When elevated into the supreme, it goes, "That pie is sure some old goo-ood!"

Some years ago one of the Popes decreed that the ancient Latinity of the Roman Catholic Church could be eased off in favor of the vernaculars, after which priests localized. But localizing had long been common practice here in Maine, an early instance concerning Loud's Island and the *Sunbeam*. The *Sunbeam* is a missionary boat that cruises up and down the Maine coast, bringing spiritual encouragement to the remote heathens of the islands and peninsulas. With no nuances of impiety, the coastal Mainers call her "God's Tugboat," and they will tell you that God's Tugboat is dedicated to benefactions that are some old goo-ood. (I must interpolate here, without relevancy, that there is a summer cruise schooner out of Penobscot Bay that is named *Victory Chimes*, but by the fishermen is called *Jingle Bells*.)

So years ago the *Sunbeam* put in at Loud's Island for a weekend, and the skipper-minister was to conduct Sunday services at the church there. The few people on the island can't support a resident parson, so the church is used only when there is a "supply," usually the *Sunbeam* skipper. Nobody goes to haul (allowed on Sunday then, but not nowadays) and everybody goes to church.

Perhaps no sacred edifice ever stood on a lovelier spot. On a decent summer Sunday, Muscongus Bay shines cerulean the compass-rose around, and the heavy flavor of bayberry and sweetfern enfolds the knoll. The catspruces of Loud's Island, as on all Maine islands, march in close order down the hill to the edge of the ocean ledges. There is no road to the Loud's Island church—people come from both ends of the island by footpaths lined with blueberry bushes, gulls overhead. The walk through the woods relaxes the communicants from their everlasting business with the sea, and they arrive in pentitent mood. There was a "goodly crowd" for the services on that Sunday morning now in context.

The nautical minister welcomed all to the warmth of Eternal Love, there was a hymn, and in time the sermon. That was indeed a magnificent Muscongus Bay Sunday, and the topic chosen for the message was fitting. It was The Creation, and the glorious beauties wrought from the darkness that was upon the face of the deep. "And the evening and the morning were the first day," the minister quoted from the Book of Genesis.

Then he said, "And God saw that it was sure some old goo-ood."

The Lard Pail

Cook said if I'd fetch her some lard, she'd make me a blueberry pie. I'd sooner have that in midwinter than a license to steal, so I brought a bag of blueberries from the freezer and went to Fales Mkt. for some lard. "No got," said Richard, who likes to toss off comical things he picks up from the summer people.

"No lard?"

"Nope."

Just to counteract his verbal sloppiness, I came back with, "Is there some reason for this deplorable destitution in a prosperous community otherwise overflowing with milk and honey?"

"My, my," he says. "I order lard all the time, but none comes."

"So how is my wife going to make me a blueberry pie?"

He pointed at several just-as-goods on the shelf. Things I had seen well recommended on the TV, all of them non-this and non-that and made from wonderful things that are good for me. I told Richard, "My wife still makes her pie crust from lard, and I have spent a lifetime keeping her in ignorance of substitutes." So I went to some other places, and at the third store I found some lard. Cook performed as agreed and the blueberry pie was delicious.

No doubt lard is scarce because demand has waned. But there is no substitute for pure leaf lard in the making of pie crust, and this should be embroidered in letters of gold and hung in every kitchen, as well as the Smithsonian Institution. Does anybody remember the lard pail?

I assume nobody remembers home-grown lard. When obsequies were held for the farm pig, the leaf fat was "tried out" in the kitchen oven and poured off as rendered into containers. Lard bought at a store might be scooped from a tub, but it also came packed in two-, three-, and five-pound tin pails—larger for hotel and restaurant use. If the lard came "loose" it would be carried home in a small pasteboard dish with some sanitation probabilities, but the lard in pails would be certainly clean. (The first lard "substitute," before Crisco and wonders, was called in all honesty a substitute, and sometimes "compound"; it's dominant virtue was a lesser price.) The lard pails were substantial, tight covers and bails, and after the lard was used the pails had a thousand uses until they wore out. The lard pail disappeared from grocery stores in the United States long ago, but for some years after that it lingered in Canada. As the symbol of Canada is the maple leaf, and this was "leaf" lard, the Canadian pails had a bright red maple leaf as a trade mark. Before the days of busing pupils to school, and before hot lunches, it was a stirring sight to look up a Canadian road and see the scholars carrying their lunches in these distinctive pails.

In my youth, before our lard pails disappeared, I had a three-pounder for my school lunch, but I was a light eater. I'd have two-three sandwiches, a cold chicken leg, pickles, cheese, cup-cakes, pie, cookies, and perhaps an apple, and then I was ready to go out and play, but most youngsters had five-pound pails. The Willard twins had a ten-pounder between them.

The lard pail was great for berrying. Slip your pants belt through the bail and have both hands free to pick. When the five-pound pail was full, it meant two quarts and a pint—"a pint's a pound the world around."

A lard pail served to take a sip of water to the biddies, and then to bring the eggs into the house.

We had a five-pound lard pail for well water. Our deep well had the best water in town, so we never put tap water on the table. A long pole had a snap on the end, and the lard pail would be lowered into the well. Just the right amount of water for a family meal. If company came, we used a pitcher, but we saw nothing gauche in having the lard pail on the table otherwise.

The lard pail was a shut-in's friend. Now and then Mother would fill a lard pail with cookies, candies, a couple of dough-nuts, maybe some fruit cake, and I'd carry it to somebody laid up, or for a birthday goodie. She'd tell me I might go inside if asked, but to mind my manners and take off my cap, and not to wear out my welcome, and always to bring back the lard pail. "I couldn't keep house without that lard pail!" she'd say.

And now people keep house without lard pails, and even without lard.

About Joe Toth

T his Joe Toth—pronounced Jo Tote—lived alone in a big sea-captain house with spacious lawns and wedding elms, and next was another big sea-captain house with lawns and elms where the Prindles lived. It was maybe seventy-five yards between the houses, and Joe was a little nearsighted. So one fine morning Joe got up at his usual hour, came down to let in the cat and start his breakfast. He sliced some bacon and laid it in a pan. He frothed two eggs in a bowl with some milk, for scrambling, and he fitted two slices of bread into the toaster. The coffee started to perk, and Joe had things in hand. Joe always ate at the big kitchen table where he could look across towards the Prindle house.

Joe was just putting some butter to his second slice of toast when he laid everything down on his plate, wiped his mouth on his napkin, pushed back his chair, and stood up.

Then he opened the back kitchen door, went through the hallway into the woodshed, crossed the woodshed to the barn, and pulled the wooden peg that served as a lock for the rolling door. Pushing on the door, Joe got it open with some protest from the rollers, and he opined to himself that he had forgotten again to squirt some oil. He now passed through the open barn door and walked down the rollway to the driveway, and stepped from the gritty gravel onto the velvety lawn. There had been a good dew, and his shoes were instantly wet. He crossed his own lawn and then crossed the lawn of the Prindles, thus coming to the back door of the Prindle barn—a hinged door that was held shut by a hook on the inside. Joe pounded on this door, and then stepped back to await a response.

It took a few minutes for Mrs. Prindle to come from her kitchen, through the shed and into the barn. When she got to the door, she lifted the hook and pushed, and there was Joe Toth standing in the morning dew.

"Good mornin', Joe," she said.

Joe said, "Good mornin'—what was it you wanted?"

"What was what that I wanted?"

"You was waving at me."

"Joe you old fool," says Mrs. Prindle, "go on back and finish your breakfast! I'm washin' my windows."

Poor New York

Back along, when New York City suffered the monstrous tragedy of getting buried with snow, I took a poll amongst the folks living here in Maine at Back River, and the question was, "If people don't like snow, why do they live in New York?" Marty Kierstead answered, "I don't know why they don't just tread 'er down, same's I do." Two people cried out in anguish, "My, my—ain't that turble!" And another said, in deep sympathy, "Ha, ha!"

On the morning of that disaster in Gotham, I awoke here in Friendship to as pretty a world as anybody has clapped an eye to in a long time. Back River, silent under winter ice, showed ripples where a light wind had frolicked with the new snow, and as I took my look a crow scaled out of the McCauley pines and started across towards Cushing where I surmised he had business. There was still some snow in the air, so as this crow

flew he gradually became absorbed and disappeared—black into a white nothing. This was not a bad thing to see before break-fast, and I rejoiced with that crow until I had neutralized a good deal of the sad news coming over my radio about New York.

There are numerous good answers to the question often asked us Mainers about what do we do in the winter. The only snow-storm difficulty I have is with my outward swinging storm door and our cat, Oboe. Not every Maine snowstorm piles up so much that I can't push this door open to let in the cat. But this one that creamed New York did it. After I made my *broche* at sight of the crow, I made some more for a snatch of pine grosbeaks, and for a pair of bluejays waiting for Oboe to get off the porch so they could tackle the crumb box. Cat lovers deplore my inhumane treatment of Oboe, who gets extinguished every evening and readmitted at matins. They haven't taken notice of the lovely antique velvet divan in my boathouse where Oboe survives my cruelty in sumptuous comfort. Her only bad moment is first thing in the morning, when she thinks it takes me altogether too long to let her in. Then, of course, I tangle with the bird lovers for having my crumb box so close to Oboe while she's waiting for me to open the door. And the morning of the New York snowstorm it took me quite a time. I had to take out a glass panel, crawl through, and go to the shop for a shovel. But once Oboe was in and had taken her morning nourishment, she stomped around with such a throbbing purr that all the picture frames went askew, and I could see that she held no resentment against me for making her sleep in the boathouse. So, other than this passing inconvenience to the cat, that snowstorm was no bother here.

I was interested when the radio told me every available truck in New York City was pressed into service to cart off the snow. In a week or so, I heard, the streets would be found again and restored to traffic. I breathed easier after that. Here in Maine we figure one truck for every hundred miles of highway, and that includes winging back for the next storm. Here at Back River I have three hundred yards of dirt driveway to clear before coming to the town road, for which I have a small garden tractor with a blower. After breakfast I blew my dooryard and driveway, and then I could go wherever I wished—except New York. I was pleased to find, when I reached the town road, that Raymond, a neighbor, had shoveled out our mail boxes, so the R.F.D. carrier could leave our letters when she came. Eleanor, our carrier (does that make her a mail lady?), is not obliged to leave anything unless our boxes are approachable, but she has been known to make exceptions. They said in New York it would take a week before mailmen could resume their appointed rounds. But here at Back River normalcy returned well before noon, and except for whittling, or painting lobster buoys by the shop stove, we had nothing to do on this beautiful Maine morning except listen to the radio and feel sorry for New Yorkers. This concerned us so much we found it difficult to remain cheerful.

Granther MacDougal

T he immutable Maine rule that the cook is boss of the lumber camp cookshack was something Granther MacDougal hadn't heard about. That's because he was a Nova Scotian. He lived near Tatamagouche, on the Toney River, at a place called Up Along, and until now he had never been farther from Up Along than Pictou. Now, he had decided in his old age to visit the Boston States and gaze for the first time on his two grandsons, Colin and Jock, who were already grown men. Neither had married. They lived with their parents, Bessie and Andrew MacDougal, Andrew being son of Granther MacDougal, and father and sons operated a sawmill at Cookson Station, Maine. So all were happy to hear that Granther MacDougal (*the* MacDougal!) would come to visit. The two grandsons told Gus Minot, their sawyer, not to get into any trouble he couldn't get out of by himself, and they drove the horse into Bangor to meet their grandfather when he arrived on the Boston-bound Maritime Express.

These two strapping grandsons looked bonny to Granther MacDougal, and they, in turn, were astonished to find the old man in the pink of good health, straight and keen, and his shoulders broad enough to toss a caber at his age. And when Granther MacDougal arrived at Cookson Station, his natural Nova Scotian appreciation of a fine woman caused him to look upon Bessie, his daughter-in-law, with extreme favor. And for good reason. Her father had been a Dillworthy from the English Midlands, by way of York County, Maine. Her mother had been an Aucoin from Berlin, New Hamp-SHEER, and Bessie had just about everything to admire. The Dillorthy influence had not, however, stifled an accent from the Aucoin, and Granther MacDougal recognized it as Acadian. It was, in fact, from Bonaventure, Baie de Chaleur. True, Bessie had long been a Mac-Dougal, and the *jooal* was muted, unless she became excited. Her clear black eyes, her straight black hair, and her bouciness of build would still suggest the Aucoin if she held back the h'acc-SENT. Granther saw she was a beautiful and able woman, and as she installed him in the spare chamber she kissed the old duffer and called him *beau-père*.

It was the third day of Granther MacDougal's visit that things began to pall and he fidgeted for lack of familiar scenes. He began to cast about for ways to amuse himself, and now while Bessie was out on the porch hanging up a wet dishcloth he came into her kitchen. She came in to find him leaning over the stove, lifting the cover of a pot so he could look into the steam and see what was cooking. He did not know, being a Nova Scotian and strange to Maine ways, that the most secure potentate that ever sat upon throne had no more power, authority, sway, and absolute jurisdiction than a Maine cook in a Maine kitchen. If that cook also has even a touch of the old Kaybeck, more so. Men who have owned a million acres of Maine timberland have known they must say yes-sir and no-sir when they eat in their own cookshacks. Granther MacDougal was intruding.

So Bessie whacked him across the back of his hand with a long-handled iron spoon. The cover of the pot jangled to the floor and the poor man hopped about the kitchen with his hand full of bees, his dignity down, and his astonishment high. When he settled down, he looked at his beautiful daughter-in-law in puzzlement, and he said, "Why did you do that?"

"Because *this* is *my* kitchen," and Bessie told him she'd thank him to keep his hands to himself and let things on the stove alone.

"But I just wanted to see what's for supper!" he whimpered.

"You ask me, I tole you—but don't touch!"

Well, the afternoon wore along and Granther MacDougal accepted things. As suppertime approached, he said, "Bessie?"

"Yes . . .

"What's for supper?"

"Vittles and with-its," said Bessie. "Ever have them up along Toney River?"

Granther MacDougal gave her a hug, and because he had learned his lesson Bessie winked at her two sons and then kissed Granther again.

The Boss's Camp

The big effort to liberate the downtrodden female surged just about the time education, as a concept, was eliminated from our public school system in favor of a unionized culture and I, if nobody else did, felt a relationship. If lovely woman stoops to the folly of equalizing herself with man, God's great mistake, she deserves what she gets. Perish the thought. It was accordingly relevant to me when the annual fund-dun letter came from my college, which had so carefully encouraged me toward enlightenment, asking if I'd need a dormitory room during commencement exercises. If so, the query ran, would I want it for one person or two people?

This person-people business stems from the Susan B. Anthony syndrome whereby sex is to be eliminated from the language and everybody will be the same. Beguiled, my college goes along. Two persons do not necessarily make a people, as in "the people of Western Europe." But the assertive ladies have wrought new thoughts such as "chairperson" and have abused the definitions. This letter came from my college the exact same day I had at last given up on "presently."

The reason I had given up on presently was a folder from a plumbing supply house with information about ". . . the pressure tanks we are now presently making at this time . . ." I didn't feel man enough to contend after that, other than to lament that our school system turns out advertising writers. I used to take folders like that and write all over them that the present tense of the verb takes care of the "now," and of "at this time," and that "presently" has nothing to do with either. So I gave up, and now at this time I am presently embracing the people-person bit.

Somewhere I acquired a sheet of sticker stamps, for putting on letters, put out by the YMCA and saying, "Send a Boy to Camp." I use one now and then, and cross out the word "boy" and write in, "person." A small remonstrance and ineffective, but a start. The difference between male and female is not political, social, psychological, and even philosophical, but strictly biological, and it was recognized by humanity and language long ago. One summer not long ago one of our Maine timberland owners agreed to participate in a university program. A group of forestry students would come to live in and study the operation of a lumber camp. When the students arrived, the group had fourteen boys and one girl. There is nothing that says a young lady can't study forestry, but there remain numerous reasons why one should not attend a lumber camp. The university had gratified the liberationists, but the camp was not yet ready for the girl who came.

The professor who was in charge of the bisexual, if top-heavy, summer program did the only thing possible—he went to the boss of the camp to suggest that arrangements be made so the young lady could have discreet accommodations in the boss's camp. No way. The boss of a camp wouldn't let God Almighty share. So, you see, the word "person" is no good if it needs another word to make it clear. Fifteen persons is not the same as fourteen boys and one girl.

It's likely, and I admit it, that Maine may resist the desexing effort longer than some places. For one thing, the word "person" usually suggests somebody not worth further identity. "Some person came to buy a pig while you were gone," wife to husband on his return.

"That so?" he says. "Nobody you knew?"

"No, just a person." And ponder the words the wife might have used to avoid "person." Gentleman? Fellow? Stranger? Perhaps character. Even "party." Mainers like party. Maybe joshing at the legal parties of the first and second part. "A party come up to me on the street . . ." Person suggests nothing in particular, but party connotes a pleasantness, a smile, maybe a laugh. A real pleasant person is sometimes called a joker. "Who's the old joker going around selling whetstones?" But I never heard joker used in Maine for a female; person, yes. And more often, party.

Well, the other day this large party in a red dress stepped up and said, "You Mr. Gould?"

I thought briefly, and somehow Ms. seemed wrong. And Miss and Mrs. didn't suit. I hardly knew what to say, but I came out with 'Yes." Then I explained to her that at our house we have become fully liberated, and we make no distinctions. Co-pers.soned. Two peoples. But he can tell, and so can she.

A Silver Sixpence

When Sarah was very young we became good friends and I made her one of my silver chests, in which she will keep her tableware if she gets any in her nuptial season. This is previous, as Sarah is still working at grade school. And presumptuous, too, the way the price of silver bounds. But if wedding guests do bring her some silverware, she has a pretty pine chest lined with green velvet to keep it in. Right now, her only piece of silver is an English six-penny coin I provided for her bridal shoe:

> Something old and something new,
> Something borrowed and something blue,
> And a silver sixpence in her shoe.

After 429 years, the British stopped coining the silver sixpence in 1980, and as I plan to make silver chests for young ladies for some time to come, I prudently laid in a supply of them while I could. For Sarah, the chest and the coin were special.

Sarah isn't like all the other good little boys and girls who wake up in the morning where they are. Sarah wakes up on an island out in Muscongus Bay, because her father is in the fisheries and has to live there. She and her younger brother begin every school day by coming to town in a boat. Then they get on a bus and ride a dozen miles. Reverse in the afternoon, except that there is a half-hour wait in the gymnasium because the bus schedule isn't worked out for islanders. Sarah's mother says this "makes for a long day."

Her mother, who would also have one of my silver chests had I known her back when she was a bride, keeps house out there on the island without many things. Electricity, for one. They do have bottled gas for cooking and refrigeration, but other kitchen conveniences won't run on bottled gas. They do have sea fogs, arctic smoke, becoming southerlies, and ships that pass. So they make out, but occasional family visits to "the main" are momentous events. My wife saw them in the stow-wer, and suggested they take the time to run over here to Back River and pick up something I had for Sarah.

Sarah's mother must have wondered what on earth I might have that belonged to Sarah, but her acceptance of the suggestion didn't hinge on that. "Goo-ood!" she said. "We'll be right ov-ver, and we'll bring the hoss-reddish!"

Knowing nothing about that meeting, I was in my woodworking shop making kindling wood, or possibly riveting a trivet, and I looked up to see Sarah standing close to watch. Lovely child. "Hello," I said, "just the one I'm looking for—I've got something belongs to you."

I brought her silver chest from under a bench, where it had been since the hot-stove season, and I dusted it off, revealing the initial "S" carved into the cover.

"Oh-h-h!" said Sarah, putting her hands to her cheeks, and then she said, "And we brought the hoss-reddish."

I would admire to leave it right there. I ought to send the reader away untold. Some things should never be explained. I recall that Charles Addams said he thought his best comic cartoons were the ones that needed no captions——but that whenever one was reprinted in Germany it always said, "This cartoon needs no caption." And one time I was driving at night in a wild rainstorm, and my automobile headlamps picked up a forlorn, and drenched, man standing at roadside. "What in the world are you doing out here on a night like this?" I asked him.

"Well," he said, "you see—I'm a piano tuner."

I wouldn't let him add a word. Anything he might say after that would spoil everything. And I'd be justified, I think, to leave sweet Sarah right there with her hoss-reddish. A raven-haired preteen beauty, the cry of gulls over tide-washed ledges, the ancient outboard being cranked to get the youngsters to school, Life on a Maine Island, serene and nonsequitur. And I said, "So you brought the hoss-reddish?"

"Eyah—Mom's got everything all ready to plug in—Oh, my! Isn't that some beautiful!" She lifted the cover and the green velvet against the honey-colored white pine made her gasp. I got the hug that is my adequate reward.

All right—I'll tell you. Mom had dug her horseradish roots out on the island, and with the customary tears had peeled and cut them. She had them in a big glass jar with the proper quantity of sharp vinegar, and she had brought the jar to the main— intending to find some way to invite herself into a home where she could plug in her electric blender and finish the job. It's not a nonsequitur at all. While Sarah and I were taking care of the silver chest, and I was getting my hug, Mom zipped the hoss-reddish.

She left some of it. It will cut a throat at thirty paces.

Always Knock First

A television commercial showed a pigtailed child running in bucolic abandon across a farm dooryard, putting a peaceful flock of biddies to flight, and I don't remember what this was supposed to sell. But I sat up at horror at this wanton dalliance and lost all attention to the product, because all farm children have always been taught never-never to frighten the hens. Makes 'em fall off, and a good hen that gets a real scare may cease to function in the nest until the stewpot takes over. I realize the commercial was thought up and produced by people who know nothing about hens, and even that the biddies may be theatrical properties kept solely for photographic purposes. But anybody who grew up with hens as I did will react my way, and I'd like to speak to that foolish kid and to the advertising agency.

The dormitoried poultry in today's agronomy don't get a chance to run at large, but on the old-time family farm the hens had the run of the place. Even out onto the road, because people who rode in buggies were careful about hens. You just didn't give a hen any kind of a startle. All hens frighten about the same, but size decides how high they fly. The feather-legged Brahmas were too beefy to soar much, but the Wyandottes and the Leghorns would squawk and cutt-cutt-cutt and fly against the barn if somebody in the next township slammed a screen door. We young ones were instructed—ordered—to move amongst the hens slowly and quietly, careful not to make sudden gestures. We were even told to speak to the birds when approaching, so they'd know we were coming.

That's right, and we always knocked on the door of the hen pen before opening it. With the door closed against the Great World, a flock busies itself in the litter, scratching and pecking while the boss men directs the work. He's the rooster. He struts and lectures, maintains dignity and order, and commands attention to the business at hand. His hens talk among themselves, and when one finds a titbit of nourishment she cutt-cutts a small announcement about it. The other biddies congratulate her, and the rooster suggests they all go and do likewise. At this moment, if a thoughtless farmer opens the door unannounced, the congenial program is interrupted and the rooster and his ladies will go right up into the air in vast surprise. So always knock on the door first. This causes the poultry to look up and nobody is alarmed when the door opens and the farmer steps in with, "Coming through, ladies!" When properly notified, the same hens that would explode into a tizzy will come to peck at the eyelets of the farmer's boots and show great friendliness. And, to the point, they will continue production and finish their clutches. A hen that doesn't lay eggs is hardly an asset.

It wasn't just hens. We didn't startle any of the stock. Nothing else would go off quite like a hen, but a horse that takes a fright may climb into his manger and be difficult to retrieve. I've seen a scared pig scale a fence. But the animals lack the pomp and hustle, the beating of wings, and the wild cutt-cutt-cutt-darking of the layers.

While meditating on that rambunctious child who scared the TV hens, I realized what ails television. It's not the poor quality and lack of taste in programming, the consuming desire for the advertising dollar, the lack of reportorial talent—it's none of those things. It's that we poor victims out front have nobody to talk to. There's nobody to listen to our complaints, to act on our advice. Who would I write to, or call, to explain about scaring hens? Were there somebody, I would freely offer, and in recompense the TV boys would have the pleasure of my friendly acquaintance. And, in this instance, I could help them a great deal. I'd tell them to get that crazy kid a flock of guinea hens.

The guinea fowls fly like a kite, going straight up, and they squeal and squawk like a lost soul with its tail caught in a door. They lay eggs, all right, but only for hatching out more guinea fowl. The egg looks like a ping-pong ball, and has never been successfully marketed as food. So it doesn't matter how much you scare a guinea hen, and she'll put on a far better show than regular hens. So put a flock of them in the petunias and trot that pigtailed child past. There's a TV commercial! And once you roust them and they're up on the roof-peak of the barn, the things will sit there all afternoon making instant replays.

On Hand Mowing

Our high school history book had a drawing of the rabble arriving in Paris for the Revolution, and the artist had equipped his army with some makeshift weapons. Prominent was a ferocious zealot brandishing a scythe, and we farm boys who were intent on cultural improvement were detoured for a moment by this absurdity. Our teacher, a country girl, agreed with us that one good man with a ball bat could probably subdue an entire regiment of handscythes. I have watched since then, and I have never seen a drawing of a handscythe that had the life. Father Time, depicted annually at year's end, always carries a strange tool with the handles askew and the snath bent the wrong way. Usually, in the cartoons, Father Time holds the handles, which are known to us experts as the *tug* and the *lug*, in such a way that should he swing the foolish thing he would mow himself off at the knees. I assume no artist has ever mowed.

My grandfather, who taught me to swing a scythe, assured me early that he had personal knowledge that the blade makes a harmless weapon. He had been privileged to watch two men fight with handscythes. When he first came upon the battle he was horrified to contemplate the consequences, but he told me he soon saw that he had nothing to dread, so he relaxed to watch the fun.

The fight was between two of his hired men. It was common talk in town that only a fool would ever work for my grandfather, and he responded by saying he had no jobs that required academic proficiency. On this occasion, he had negotiated with

Dunky Ross and Ho-ho Blaisdell, two worthies who completely satisfied the common talk in town, and he had set them to mowing swalegrass. Our hillside farm had "runs" in the fields, gullies that drained the land. They stayed wet in dry weather so could not be mowed by machine. Vegetation in these runs went to reeds and rushes and sweetflag and cattails and wasn't good for hay to feed out. It could be used for bedding or for mulch. It had to be cut each summer or in time the runs, or swales, would invade the fields. So there was no profit in swalegrass and Gramps spent as little as possible on it. Dunky and Ho-ho came cheap because of their arrested intelligence, and when Gramps got them swinging in the swales he went over the knoll to pick tomatoes.

As soon as he was out of sight, Dunky and Ho-ho, who were not so foolish as some people thought, repaired to the farmhouse and went "down sulla" to refresh themselves at my grandfather's barrel of cider. When they returned to the swale, they were feeling nicely, and some philosophical remark of Dunky prompted Ho-ho to a scholarly disagreement. One thing led to another, tempers flared, and shortly the two were dueling each other courageously with their handscythes. When my grandfather came by with a wagonload of tomatoes, Dunky and Ho-ho were jumping about and yelling a good deal, slapping with their scythes, and Gramps hustled from the wagon seat to intercede before the slaughter got too far out of hand. But he told me he saw at once that while a handscythe would seem to make a formidable snickersnee, it is nonetheless so hung and so shaped that it is neither lethal on a thrust nor difficult to parry. So, deciding that Dunky and Ho-ho were in no mortal danger, he went back to the wagon seat to watch the conflict as if it were a game of horseshoes. After the two heroes simmered down, they slept off the cider under a tree, Gramps fired them and mowed the swales himself to save three dollars.

As hand mowing has waned in deserved desuetude, I have continued to practice the art—partly because Gramps taught me the right way and scything is not the hard work it appears to be if you know the right way. I devote a few minutes each morning in August to mowing our window-view of Back River. I don't make hay, as our shore runs to bayberry, sweetfern, hardhack, wild roses, and goose greens—about as valuable as swalegrass. My wife thanks me when I have covered the area, and the scythe is put away until next year. And when I hang it over the beam in the shop I notice again the curious hang and the improbable shape, and I think about the French Revolution and about Dunky and Ho-ho. I wonder how far that Revolutionist got into the City of Paris before some Loyalist lammed him with a sledstake.

About Seeing Snakes

W hen the McCauleys come from out-of-state to tent on their Maine coast property here at Back River, I always hoist the John Paul Jones jack on my flagpole by way of welcome. That's the flag with the rattlesnake and the motto Don't Tread On Me, used during the American Revolution. Dr. McCauley is a herpetologist, and with this flag prominent we consider him properly greeted in his own language. After their tent is up Rob and Lois spend much of their vacation viewing the fauna along Back River, and as Rob is a wildlife specialist he never has to look in a book to tell a widgin from a whistler. A couple of mornings after they were set up I asked Rob about my snakes. "How come I am seeing so many more snakes this summer than in previous years?" I asked.

It would be imprudent to ask that of anybody except a herpetologist. My rude and comical local cronies would just tell me to lay off the sauce, or ask if I'd seen any butter-colored whipsnakes with green stripes and hard hats, and so on and so forth. In popular lore, snakes go with tippling. But, a professional snake authority, such as Dr. McCauley, will give serious thought and a scholarly answer. Rob now laid down his binoculars, assumed an academic posture, touched his fingers, pursed his lips, and although he was on vacation he cocked his head in thought. Not everybody who sees snakes can apply to an expert, so I was eager to hear his reply. "Well," he said, "have you considered the possibility that you simply have more snakes this summer?"

That had not occurred to me, as I supposed the snake count is constant, and it goes to show that an education is a fine thing. Rob told me these Maine, and nonvenomous, snakes are garter snakes, something I can't figure unless it derives from garden, since I see my snakes while they are haunting my garden and protecting my sass from the ravage and depredations of my hoppy-toads. I don't mind having the snakes on duty, as I am aware they devour some unfriendly bugs and beetles, but they are hard on hoppy-toads, which also devour unfriendly bugs and beetles. As my snakes increase, my hoppy-toads decline. It is Mother Nature's way. Herpetology as a study includes both, so Dr. McCauley is indifferent and views reptiles and amphibians broadly.

I take notice that I have had a lonely garden life since knowledge of my snake increase has reached the neighborhood. The ladies, in particular, are reluctant to socialize as they used to do amongst the peas and cukes. Time was I would say, "Come, see my garden!" and the ladies would walk up and down the rows admiring. Then I would reward them with a head of lettuce or a snatch of carrots, and it made for pleasant discourse and amiability. Then it happened.

"Would you like a cauliflower?" I called, and the lady said, "Oh, I would *love* a cauliflower," and she strode down the row past the peppers and pole beans to where I was opening my jackknife. Then:

GEE-EE-EE-EE-EE-EEK!

Even the most confirmed misogynist must admire the grace, charm, celerity, and agility, as well as the basic intent, of a sedate

lady who, with cream cauliflower in context, suddenly *Eeks!* and clears the pumpkin patch at one bound to climb up on the woodpile. "Gracious!" I said. "Whatever *is* the matter?"

"A snake!"

I cultivated this potential. "Would you like a cauliflower?" I called, and it worked quite a few times. Then came Mrs. Potter, who caught me up short.

"Would you like a cauliflower?" I called.

Mrs. Potter said, "Oh, I would *love* a cauliflower!" So I started to take out my knife, and I heard her say, "My, those are certainly some handsome peppers!" Then when she didn't say anything more, I looked up, and there was Mrs. Potter holding my best snake by the scruff of the neck and looking into his beady eyes. "Garter snake," she said. "Three years old, I'd say."

"Dr. McCauley says four."

"He's probably right, but I'd say three. Handsome male."

I did ask Dr. McCauley when he was here as to why my snakes favored the cucumbers in the morning and the onions in the afternoon. He said about anything a snake does is to enhance the metabolism, which sounds about right if you trouble to think it over. Lacking herpetological expertise, I had erroneously concluded it wasn't metabolism so much as it was the hoppy-toads. For some reason the hoppy-toads like afternoon onions, and snakes are never so keen on onions as they are on hoppy-toads.

Always Uphill

A News item tells us the Meddle Department of the United States government has required the J. C. Penney people to call back a batch of bicycles. Something about these bicycles can come apart, and Uncle Sam is fearful people might get hurt. This may be a laudable function of today's bureaucratic Omnisciency, but it doesn't make sense in my recollections of boyhood bicycles. If J. C. Penney is putting out a bicycle that threatens the flesh and bones of the kiddos, J. C. Penney should get an A-plus for perpetuating the honest American traditions.

I never had a bicycle that didn't come apart several times a day, always with dire disaster, and if there came a day nothing broke it made talk about the neighborhood. True, this was a bit ago. Just this summer a mother down the road told me she had a deal on with her young son—every dollar he earned she was matching with two dollars, and he was "working" on a bicycle. I never had a deal like that and I never earned a dollar. I earned money, but never a dollar. I mowed the lawn for one sea cap-

tain's widder-woman, and she paid me ten cents an hour. I could mow her lawn in an hour. But if I hustled and finished the lawn in fifty minutes, she'd pay me but eight cents. I had quite another way to work on a bicycle.

I found my frame on the town dump. It had a twisted front fork, suggesting it had moved the immovable object, and also explaining why it was on the town dump. There was no problem. I stuck the thing in the big vise at Charlie Dunning's blacksmith shop, and Charlie ran a length of iron pipe over the bent part and yanked back a certain amount of originality. He didn't get it all, as he felt he might break something, so my bike had a list to starboard and I was never able to ride it no-handsies. But he did get the fork so the cones of a wheel would line up, and now I had to go and find a wheel. Thaddy Buker had one with eight broken spokes. It didn't just rub; it bound up. But I could get spokes for it, so I gave Thaddy fifteen cents and took the wheel. Then I had to mow some lawns to get money enough to buy new spokes at the bicycle shop in the city. I tried to stretch the widder-woman's lawn into twelve cents, but she shook her head and said she never paid more than ten cents.

I was lucky with the rear wheel. I found an old kitchen range buried under pine needles in the woods, probably all that was left of a chopper's camp, and I carried the pieces home one by one until I had them all. About a mile. Then Benjy Gartley, who bought junk, took them and gave me a perfectly good hind wheel, coaster brake and all. It was perfect, except that it was smaller than my front wheel, and I always rode uphill.

The frame had a crack, which spread shortly and became a break. I couldn't fix it until it broke off, so I rode around some in the constant expectation of taking a header when it let go. I did, and then I fixed it. I shoved a piece of water pipe on over the break, so the break was in the middle, and then I bored holes for rivets. Charlie Dunning, good friend of all us boys, gave his approval and said the job would last for years. Good as new.

Tires were a problem. None, then, had inner tubes, and each was shellacked to its rim. Had to stick them on, because if they moved on the rim the valvestems would tear out. When a tire sprang a leak, which every tire did, it was a major operation to get the wheel out of the fork, the tire off the wheel, and everything back again. So the make-do was to wind friction tape around the leak, wheel and all. This kept the Neverleek from oozing, and a wound-around tire would hold air sometimes. Neverleek was a patent product that came in a tube. The tube was threaded to fit the valvestem of a tire, and the tube of Neverleek was squeezed in. After that, if a tire leaked, it leaked Neverleek, and the tape helped stop that. Neverleek looked like molasses, and may have been. What I saved on new tires I spent for Neverleek and friction tape.

All of which was attended constantly by the J. C. Penney hazard Uncle Sam is now hoping to abate. Things did fall apart, and bicycling taught us how to fall at high speed and slide forty yards on the back of the neck. What would fine old Uncle Sam know about the abrasive quality of a cinder sidewalk of my youth, which would shred a pair of corduroy pants in a split second? And so we boys would pick ourselves up, and then pick up the separated parts of our bicycles, and we would carry them home in our arms. Now to find replacements, to dicker, to mow some more lawns, and then be back in business for the next disaster.

Funny thing, and probably J. C. Penney and Uncle Sam don't know this, but after the high-wheeled bicycle, the new kind was called a "safety." The safety eliminated the dangers and disadvantages of the old high-wheeler. I still heard the word "safety" for a bicycle when I was a boy, meaning a bike just like mine. And what would Uncle Sam do about the grave dangers of the carbide lamp? A little can of carbide and a drip of water made a gas that burned with bright white light, and on the front of a bicycle this shone enough so night riding was reasonably safe. Marty French's carbide bicycle lamp blew up on him and took the side off his father's barn.

The Noisy Woods

S ome poet named Raymond Henri undoubtedly composes in an urban environment, and he has favored us with some verses called "Silence in a Wood." He enlarges on the dearth of noises in a forest, assuming as city slickers are wont to do that there in the sylvan dell and the bosky copse the whine of the fire engine and the shrill whistle of the policeman and the honking and grinding of traffic are lacking, so everything is quiet. He tells us, poetically, that the faint rustle of leaves stirring in the breeze are "sighs." Before I finish, I plan to explain about one of those sighs. No doubt the delusion that the countryside is peaceful began with ancient Horace, whose city mouse bemoaned the rural lack of "crowds and stir." Pshaw! Give me the hardened city-ite who can sleep with his apartment window open against the hullabaloo of torrential traffic—one who snores through jackhammers and buses shifting gears—and I'll stick him in a bedroll by a wooded dell and prove that a bug-eyed insomniac can be made in one boisterous night. There's little silence in a "wood."

Well, it isn't a wood—it's "the woods." One goes into the woods and one comes out of the woods. You can't see the woods for the trees. The woods is full of them. And if you think that delicate little sigh is the murmuring of rustling leaves, be assured it's far more than that—it's the turn of the tide. A hundred miles from the ocean the message comes. And if the night is fairly quiet, this sigh will waken any sleeper whose ear is tuned. The force involved is truly astronomical—sun, moon, the universe, the oceans, a vast movement. Far away, somewhere, whatever it is that swings the stupendous pendulum will hit the cycle on the button, and everything that was going that-a-way will turn and go this-a-way. The incredible suction that begins is by no means a coastal matter. Farmhouse windows far from the tide will have the curtains stir as the air shifts, a dying fire on a hearth will puff some smoke, a shed door may squeak on a rusty hinge, and the poplar leaves will stir. People who understand will say, "Tide turned!" and it is so. But hardly a sigh; it is a gasp, a heave, a gulp, and it throws into reverse a force immeasurable.

But the turn of the tide, so far from the ocean, is a sound that is truly perceived rather than heard. There are other sounds like that—the drumming of a bull partridge is one. As part of his matrimonial affairs, the cock grouse will stand on tippy-toe and begin to beat his wings against his body. Slowly, he beats faster, and in the end is making a whirr. In the woods, it sounds like a drum beat developing into a flourish. And when afar, it sounds perhaps close by; when near, it seems at a distance. And if you are a poet and have never heard a grouse before, you will probably assume somebody is trying to start the reluctant motor on a camp water pump, perhaps on a lawn mower. It is possible, if you approach with care, to creep up on a pa'tridge in this absurdity. When he gets through thumping himself, he seems to be punchy, and in need of a good rest. Stay still with patience, and you can watch him get ready again and go through the foolishness another time. His wife is somewhere around, sitting on a nest of eggs.

The noises of the woods never keep a woodsman awake. But take somebody out of the madding crowd and stick him in a tent up-river! The embers of the campfire have been covered with wet pine needles to make a smudge that will entertain the mosquitoes, and the whine of the mosquitoes is noticeable. The frogs along the stream are croaking splendidly now, and up the bog a stake-driver is pounding out his goodnight cal-ooooomps in rhythmic delight. The guide, who has taken this chap on his vacation, is now well asleep, lulled by the woodland sounds he knows so well. The surge of the waterfalls just upstream plays background to all else, a drop of maybe fifteen feet that orchestrates the twilight with the enthusiasm of a Niagara. Swooping to investigate the frogs, a dusty hooty-owl fetches up to perch in a pine and go hoot-toot-hoot-toot-hoot-toot-hoot-toot for a half hour, being pleasantly answered hoot for toot by a friend back in the timber. If the owls subside, then can be heard the loon in the lake above the waterfalls as she berates her husband in the manner of a Middle Ages heretic being boiled in oil. His reply usually brings the chaps from the city to a sitting posture. Oh, did poet ever lie listening to the noises of the woods and wonder what is out there in the leaves? 'Tis a bunny rabbit, and now, just for fun, he kicks his hind legs on the ground. Thump!

Or, has poet ever heard a pair of porcupines making love in the upper branches of a tree? Sometimes they talk politics, too. They make an incredible bedlam of sound, squawks and squeals, grunts and groans. Midnight is about right. Most people hearing porkies for the first time refuse to believe it's porkies, and think bears. But bears sound more like loons, and do their yelping on the run along the ridges, so there is a crashing noise, too.

One of the really good noises in the woods is that of a bull moose coming to splash in the stream. From the bedroll, the sound approaches and is cumulative, like a Central Vermont freight train coming down the White River Valley. It always seems to be headed straight for the bedroll. First, the poet will hear the cracking of twigs, and then the snapping of limbs as the monster runs into spruce trees. The thunder of hoofs. When the beast reaches the stream, he does his splashing, and in good time returns to his business up on the ridge. Now would be the time for the poet to arise, light the gasoline lantern, which hisses incredibly, and set down his wing-ed words about the silences of the forests.

No good night in the woods is perfect without a treesqueak. Perhaps all the other noises have been absorbed or endured, and the poet at long last is about to slumber. The treesqueak is an aggregate of demons, fays, trolls, kobolds, and poltergeists that sits up in a tree and rubs two limbs together. A small breeze suffices, but things are better with a wind. Just when a tree-squeak gets doing his best, along comes a raccoon that tips all the tin dishes into the water pail. Oh, yes—sometimes a pair of flying squirrels will entertain. They make little slapping noises when they land. The porkies are still at it.

Poems about silence in the woods are made by poets who have never been there.

Season's Knell

Some years ago a lady reader wrote to ask if the seasonal flights are led by a goose or a gander—probably because she was curious, since this was before the Equal Rights Amendment was thought up. I answered the letter, but not the question—geese are like the happy, bounding flea and even close by the beholder is dubious. When a flock passes over, the keenest eye will see little difference. I stood this morning (as I wrote) and watched a flock of Canada geese lift off our Back River and move with great cry into the day's formation, and I smiled about that woman's letter.

'Tis a brave sight. Our Back River must have some feed for migrating geese, but I'd sooner think they come in here to rest. Our Canada goose nests, or has been known to nest, within the United States to the west'ard, but those we see on our Atlantic flyway in the fall are heading south for the winter all the way down from the Arctic and sub-Arctic and the gaggles are in great number. I'd guess maybe two-three hundred in this flock this morning. The hullabaloo of the takeoff will beguile the viewer to the exclusion of minor details, so I watched in sexless admiration. A goose is a goose. And I doubt if it matters and I doubt if anybody knows.

From my observations, a flight of geese seems to have a constant shift of command. These flocks that visit me overnight have come a long way. The Gaspé, Baie de Chaleur, at least from Prince Edward Island. It was a long day, and they are tired. There seems to be organization, but there also seems to be confusion. There's a lot of talk, as if weighty matters were being discussed. This eases off during darkness, although some chatter goes on all night, and then in the morning we hear the volume gain again. Just before takeoff the honking swells, and since there must be a leader, whatever signal he or she gives is made against a considerable tumult. With great splash and honking and co-honking, the flock rises from one side, so the last to fly have waited a time. But the takeoff is nonetheless all together and all at once, and off they go in a total disarray. They rend our dooryard with whoop and halloo because they aren't more than ten yards above our rooftop. They rise quickly, however, and are well in the air in a minute or so. The honking fades, but we can still hear it after the birds have disappeared into the south.

There comes a point when the chorus suggests a lonely hound baying the moon.

But during this takeoff and before any flight pattern is formed, a flock seems to have no particular leader. There is jockeying for position. A bird on ahead will fall back; one behind will move up. And even after the classical V begins to shape up, there is changing here to there, back and forth. There seems to be doubt in the first airborne minutes as to which goose should fly where. I surmise flying geese take turns being leaders.

And while 'tis, indeed, a brave sight—there is a sadness. The departure of the Canada goose is the knell of the season. They have their way of knowing, which the Whether Bureau does not, and one day they are gone and the next day we have ice in Back River. Up they rise and off they go, and the wind shifts. Put away the lawn mower and take down the snow shovel. Summertime friends. But as they honk and rise, they make their promise—when the ice is gone and the air is warm and the grass is greening, they will be back.

So they will. When next I hear a honk, male or female I wot not, I'll probably be planting the sweet peas. That will be nice.

Putting Us On?

A goodly bunch of us boys was in Marty Potter's barber-shop and close shave emporium the other forenoon, and I was in the chair when Goopy Groober, the town cop, stuck his head in the door and said, "You open today, huh?"

"I'm open," said Marty.

"Good," said Goopy, "I'll noise it up and down the street."

"I shall be everlastingly grateful," said Marty, and I said, "What was all that about?"

But before Marty could expatiate in his customary horticul-
tural verbosity (flowery language), the door opened and in came
Randy Oliver to say, "You're open today, eh?"

Marty nodded and said, "Take a seat and I shall attend to
your heart's desire in a prompt and efficient manner ere long."

"Where was you all day Monday, Tuesday, Wednesday, and
Thursday?" asked Randy. "I came by to get a haircut and the
door was locked and nobody knew where you were."

"That's right," said Marty.

"Well, where was you?"

"I been wondering about that, too," said Rufus Toothaker. "I
needed a haircut bad for the church supper, and had to go to
the thing looking like a busted bale of hay."

Father Everett Greene, retired vicar of St. Andrew's Church,
laid down his crossword puzzle at that and said, "I noticed at
the church supper that you needed a haircut, but I understood,
because I've been trying to get one myself during this prolonged
hiatus." He turned to Marty and said, "Did you enjoy your
vacation?"

Marty snipped about my ear for a time before he answered,
and then he chose his words and he said very slowly, "I am the
unwilling victim of bureaucratic interpretation. I am not allowed
to keep my shop open for the convenience of my customers and
the good of the public in general—if I do, the Social Security
people say I'm working too much and they cut off my gravy.
I've done my best to explain to them that I'm not necessarily
working or making money just because my shop is open; I tell
them a good part of my time is spent sitting around waiting for
trade. I've read that 1938 *Reader's Digest* so many times I wake
up in the night repeating the articles. But I make no headway at
all—long's the hasp is undone on the screen door I'm stuck. So
I've got to close up to keep them happy, and it so happens that
I'm available this morning. If you don't like my arrangement, go
tell the Social Security people."

"They told me it was earnings," said Randy. "I got to tell 'em
how much I earn, but they don't ask me how long it took to earn
it."

"True, true," said Marty. "But you speculate and work under your hat. You don't have a shop with a front door on it and the hours posted."

"Funny thing," said Father Greene, "that this subject should come up in my presence. I am involved in it to a very special degree, even more than Marty. I can assure you that Marty is perfectly justified in a closing down his butchery to mollify the absurdities of the bureaucracy."

"Now you're just making fun of me," said Marty.

"Not at all," said Father Greene. "You see, when I became a senior citizen and retired from the altar, I was immediately accorded the generous benefits of governmental largesse. I got my first check and it pleased me a great deal. Then I got a print-out communication telling me I had to go to the Social Security office and explain my situation. The young man asked me if I prayed very much.

Father Greene paused, and then went on. "I said yes, that I did. I said I had got into the habit during the years of my priesthood, and that it was not an easy thing to desist now that I was retired. The young man seemed astounded at this, and he told me I would have to stop praying altogether. He said that praying, with me, was work, and as long as I wanted to draw my benefits I'd have to be retired completely. Strange consequence when it's a federal offense to pray."

"Your putting me on," said Marty.

Father Greene said, "I am?"

Garden Surprise

One of the seed catalogs offers a special packet described as "Grandmother's Garden," and says it has a surprising mixture of old-fashioned country flowers such as grandmotherpeople grew back on the farm. It might be so. My grandmother had a flower garden that was full of surprises, and a memorable one was when she surprised a Brahma hen that was taking a quiet dusting in the petunias. That was a big day on the farm. The Brahma is a heavy breed with feathers up and down the legs, and this old biddy was a whopper. Somehow she got over the little stick fence around the flower garden, which was meant to keep hens out, and she was rolling and kicking behind the pumple-stone border of the petunias in the fluffing luxury hens generate when they find a good place to dust. Grandmother came out of the house with a frying pan full of greasy wash water. The frying pan had just processed a galaxy of pork chops for the haying crew, so this wash water was real fatty.

The disposal system of our farmhouse at that time consisted of a lead gooseneck pipe that ran from the kitchen sink through the wall of the house and ended in midair about a foot beyond. Sink water, when released, next fell into a wooden trough—two boards nailed together in a V—and was conveyed to a point between the grapevine and the egg plum tree, where it perpetuated a damp place where we could find fishing worms in dryest times. The cesspool and septic tank had not yet been imagined. So that gooseneck was all the plumbing we had, and it was not

prudent to slop fatty and soapy water down the gooseneck, since that could foul the drain and it would certainly build up a mess in time. So Grandmother was now taking the frying pan of greasy water to dump it off in the field somewhere. Frying pan in hand, she found this brazen Brahma lallygagging in the petunias.

Grandmother let out a yell that lifted the straw hats off the haymakers up in the far field, and she hove the frying pan at the hen. The greasy water missed very few things. The frying pan clanged one by one on the pumple stones, and picked up a resounding vibration so it scaled over the hen's head like a cathedral carillon. Taken unawares, while every feather was relaxed in the delight of the soft garden dust, the hen thought the sky was falling and began to trot around like the charge at Balaklava calling attention to imminent destruction. She tread down the soapy flowers and soaked up a lot of pork chop grease. This hoss-trot made Grandmother yell some more, and her vituperation and calumny resounded for miles around. One would never suppose there was all that much that one woman could think up to say to a hen.

After the Brahma had flattened the verbena, hollyhocks, calen-doo-las, coreopsis, salvia, and all the other pretty flowers in Grandmother's Garden, including the "yarbs," she scaled the stick fence and followed a southerly course. That was the best surprise in Grandmother's Garden, ever.

The frying pan lay on the ground and quivered for five minutes.

No Lady, He

S portswriters and sportscasters continue to try, and now we have an athlete who "has great self-confidence in himself." And another who plays basketball "like the textbook says." Oh? Like which textbook says? Seems, too, that all of Babe Ruth's records have been broken except one. That's most innings pitched in one game. But the fellow didn't tell us how many innings or which game, and if Ruth won or lost. You could look it up. So, the athletes at our Bangor High School are known as The Rams, and they play other high schools called the Falcons, and The Tigers, and The Bobcats, and so on in the esoteric lingo of the sporting trade. Well, the girls basketball team of Bangor High School played South Portland High School girls for the state championship, and the radio man came up with an interesting switch—The Lady Rams.

Perhaps some eager Woman's Libber will volunteer to tell us if this is considered a gain or a loss in the crusade. Nobody who knows anything about rams would think in the feminine. We were always leery of our buck sheep and kept an eye on them, so over the years scarcely anybody got killed, but even with perpetual *en garde* somebody would now and then get tumbled into the rhubarb with his dignity askew. If small children were to be about, we kept Aries tethered or penned, but resident farm youngsters ran a constant risk and never gave a butter an even break. Old Butthead would mostly roam the dooryard and barnyard, a necessary asset to be tolerated and avoided. "Avoid" is a good word, because when a ram charges he lowers his head and stays on target, and if the target moves he doesn't adjust. He just keeps on going, and by the time he pulls up to turn and take another aim, you can be gone.

Before my time, contributing to family lore, we had a hired man who turned a dirty trick on Aunt Vashti, a maiden lady of unsmirched character and stately aplomb. The evil deed was not done a-purpose. This hired man was on his way to harness Fan (a lady stallion), and was about to open the door of her boxstall to fetch her out when the ol' Butthead of that era caught him fair and square in a fundamental manner, wreaking astonishment and pain. Being delighted that he had connected, the ram backed off to try again and dug his hoofs into the barn floor to get a good start. There happened to be a bushel basket handy, and in a smart maneuver the hired man grabbed this up and shook it in a manner to give the ram something to aim at.

The ram did take aim at it, and lowered his head and charged. The hired man now stepped nimbly aside and slipped the basket on over the ram's head *en passant*. The ram, basket and all, smashed into the wall of Fan's stall so she whinnied and was high-strung all day, and the hired man made his escape, returning later to harness Fan.

After that, this hired man made a practice of keeping empty bushel baskets within reach, and several times saved his life in this manner. The few seconds it took ol' Butthead to get himself out of a basket were sufficient. But this conditioned the ram so he developed a great hatred for bushel baskets, and if he found one sitting around innocently he would charge it and butt it all

over the place. Nobody knew how the hired man had wrought this, so everybody wondered about the battered and abused bushel baskets found in the most improbable places.

Then Aunt Vashti dyed her yarn. She had washed the fleeces (from lady rams, mostly), carded and spun, twisted and skeined, and had dipped into the colors in the big iron kettle. Red, green, blue—she had everything ready in a bushel basket and was going to hang the skeins on the barnyard fence to finish drying and to let the colors "set."

The details need not be enumerated. Aunt Vashti survived the first skirmish and climbed to the safety of the hayrack. She forgot her sedate and ladylike reputation and delivered great villification upon the ram. He (the ram) paid no special heed to her comments, but continued to butt the basket until all the yarn was unwound and the barnyard was a bower of beauty, a rainbow and galaxy of color. The hired man was contrite, and explained matters. In conclusion, and pertinent to this discussion, in Aunt Vashti's entire harangue from the hayrack, during which she covered everything that can be applied to a ram, never once did she refer to ol' Butthead as a "lady."

Only if Funning

Other people would go to milk a cow, but my father would sometimes announce, "Alas! I shall now wend my weary way o'er the plod and extract the lacteal fluid from the bovine!" Considering his meager public schooling, Dad had a fine vocabulary and he liked to fool around with words. His pompous verbosity was wholly a spoof, because he couldn't abide people who "put on airs" and used big words to show off without trying to be funny. "Why can't he talk like a human being?" he'd ask. His stilted periphrastics, amusing himself and others, may have been a reaction to the Gothics his mother used to read aloud to the family in the kerosene lamplight. And he may have been thinking about instructing us children, maybe like reversing a backfield. There was one precious evening that we sat at table harking to his lecture on being simple and direct in conversations, and then he said, "All right—now go ahead and ingest your crepuscular nourishment!"

He used one remark often, and it does sound like a Gothic. It was his way of greeting somebody who surprised him. He might be splitting wood behind the barn to look up and see an old friend approaching. He'd sink the ax in the block, stride forward with outstretched hand, and say, " 'What ho!' ejaculated the angry monarch in fine scorn!" We youngsters had no idea where he got it, but it did sound like the *Castle of Otranto*, and we appreciated that it was permitted to talk like that if you were funning. Otherwise, his customary hello to somebody would be, "Greetings and salutations!"

He came into the house one day to say to Mother, "Madam Dufarge, your larndry is satisfac-tor-ially desiccated." I couldn't find any of that in the dictionary, partly because I've never known how to spell desiccated, but it did make me go and look. There's nothing wrong with that. Whenever somebody came into our yard who should be invited to descend and enter the house, Dad would call, "Extricate the quadruped!" Even after automobiles he called that, because in his youth unhitching the horse meant a longer visit, not just a dooryard call. It was part of a longer thing attributed to an old Quaker who wanted his horse taken care of overnight: "Extricate the quadruped from the vehicle, stabulate him, and when the early hour of morn doth arrive thee shalt be amply rewarded for thine amiable hospitality." Dad could as well have said, "Welcome! Come in!" but then we children wouldn't have known so much about words. He used to tell about the woman with Mrs. Malaprop tendencies who "instructed a condition on her homicide so she could ascertain more hostilities."

At our table the vinegar cruet was always "the Widder Cruse's oil bottle." When Dad asked for the Widder Cruse's oil bottle, we passed him the vinegar cruet. It was a big day when, somewhat later, I read I Kings:17 and found Elijah the Tishbite consoling the poor widow at the gate of the city. I came to know the Widder Cruse! My sister and I had the chore of "doing" the supper dishes, and child-fashion we'd dilly and dally so the sink was often occupied when Dad came from the barn to wash up.

Our dishpan accordingly became the "crucible of time." Cutting firewood was "manufacturing arboreal fuel." When he plucked a chicken he was "defoliating some nourishment." Not all his pet ones were puns, but he did have some—his big maul for driving stakes for barbed wire was his "weapon of defense."

When he bought the big house where we children were to grow up, there came with it a cast-off black walnut living room set that had been forgotten long ago up under the eaves in the barn chamber. The upholstery had tattered away long since, but the wood was as beautiful as ever. One day Dad opened the trap door and passed the several pieces of this set down through to my mother, who reached up to take them. With new upholstery the set was magnificent, and Mother proudly kept it in the parlor ever after. Everybody who came into the room admired it, for it was truly worthy of being in a museum. One day somebody looked at it and said. "Is the set a family antique?"

Dad kept a straight face, so my mother and we children kept straight faces. It wasn't easy. We all understood as we heard him that words are wonderful things and will do just about anything you want of them. We heard our father say, "Yes, it is—it was handed down to my wife."

Cuddly and Happy

S omebody with, I'm sure, nothing else to do, and probably on a fat government grant, has just done a scholarly survey to reveal to society that it costs more to keep a man in jail than it does to put a boy through college. There was a vague inference, not exactly proved but waiting to be pounced on eagerly by our money-hungry educators, that we wouldn't have so many men in jail if we put more boys through college. This interesting juxtaposition of jail and college gives me a chance to advance a contention of mine of long standing—that everything would be much better off if every young man were required to fetch up a calf. It is an experience that teaches everything, and compared to jail and college is dirt cheap. You even make a penny. The companionship should begin when the calf is brand new, on his wobbles, and his mother is mooing softly as she laps him. He (this is a boy calf) is a gladsome thing. If Dad happens to think you old enough, smart enough, and big enough, he will say, "Want to raise him up?" Oh boy! You're in business. Later that day you take your very own calf down to the end of the tie-up, and friendship begins. He has some clean straw to lie on, and a string around his neck to a ring in the wall, so he can visit his mother only when you let him. That first night, come the right time, you do release him, and you help his still wobbly legs bring him along the tie-up to the parent stem. He knows just what to do, and his Mommie turns to moo at him. When he is fed, new milk on his chops, you wibble-wobble him back to his little bed of clean straw and make his string fast to the ring in the wall. He is grateful, and he is cuddly and happy. As the proud owner of a new calf, you pat him, stroke him, and when you go to bed you think about him, and after you get to sleep you dream about him, and when you wake he's on your mind.

But during the night the wibble-wobbles have gone. You find your calf straining at his string, as if to pull the ring out of the wall, aimed at his mother. When you untie the string, he bolts, and there is no strength in your boyish arms to hold him. So you go sliding along the tie-up on your belly, too scairt to let go the string. By the time you pick yourself up, not too tidy, he has tackled Mommie, had his breakfast, and full of rowdy-dow is ready to disport and cavort. He is all lightning bolts, explosions, national disasters, and hoopla. Education is now coming along just fine and so far it hasn't cost a nickel, bailiff or bursar. Getting him back to his straw takes more smart than passing algebra, and more sweat than a Rose Bowl game—or a rock pile.

Besides, Rose Bowl games come but once a year, and Gulliver (I just named him Gulliver) has to get to Mommie twice a day or he'll tear down the barn and Mommie will blat up a storm. It is incredible how much that calf is going to teach that boy in the next few weeks.

And one of the world's greatest educational experiences comes when Gulliver is ready to be removed completely and permanently from Mommie, and is going to eat and drink on his own so that Mommie's bounty can be sold to the creamery. There is no more magnificant surprise in a boy's life. Our little student brings a pail of warm skimmed milk from the kitchen, into which a couple of handfuls of calf meal have been stirred with a stick. He now approaches Gulliver, who has no idea what a pail of warm skimmed milk is, with calf meal stirred with a stick, and he has no suspicion that he is about to be taught how to drink from a pail. He thinks he is going to be released again, and is taut on his string aimed at Mommie. Mommie now moos to encourage him. It is not to be. Our boy now sticks two fingers of his left hand into Gulliver's mouth and Gulliver, frantic with hunger, is beguiled into thinking he has found Mommie. He makes an effort to draw milk from the boy's two fingers. When he gets to working properly on the fingers, not yet aware that he is mistaken, the boy lowers his hand into the pail of warm skimmed milk into which a couple of handfuls of calf meal have been stirred with a stick. Suddenly Gulliver finds milk between the fingers, and with gurgles of delight goes to work in earnest. What is taking place here is top-notch instruction in agronomy, economics, subsistence, and merchandising. Gulliver is coming along, and he must be adjusted to the family program. Just as soon as he learns to drink from a pail the money coming from Mommie's milk will buy a good deal more than calf meal. Simple as that. The boy understands. And now Gulliver is drawing very well on the two fingers, and is guzzling milk and calf meal, and it is time to withdraw the boyish fingers and leave Gulliver on his own.

It happens every time. Just as the boy is about to take out his fingers, Gulliver, in the ecstacy of gustatory delight, lets go a snort of joy and appreciation, and he blows a good deal of that nice, warm skimmed milk with calf meal up the boy's sleeve and under his armpit. It spreads out in friendly stickiness to ooze along inside his shirt, to run down along his underwear, and to drip out of his pants into his shoes. Gulliver, however, you will notice, is now well instructed in drinking from a pail, and finishes his breakfast. This is all educational for boy and calf, and nutritious to Gulliver.

After that come the weeks of careful attention, bedding down, cleaning out, brushing, and one day there are little buttons where Gulliver is gong to have horns. He looks like a comer. Other boys, raising calves, come to inspect him and compare notes. Gulliver has to be kept ready at all times for such visits, and education goes on. Whatever becomes of Gulliver, you owe him a great deal for the way he has instructed you and brought you along in understanding and discipline. You will never forget your first calf. He kept you out of mischief, lessening your risk of jail. And whatever you finally do with Gulliver—veal, auctioned at the fair, baby beef, maturity—there'll be a penny coming in to help with college.

I made no survey and I had no government grant. Just an opinion. If every boy brings up a calf, we might need fewer colleges, and perhaps no jails at all.

With the Wind

A nugget of didacticism in the old Chatauqua days had to do with the three laborers digging a ditch with picks and shovels. A man comes by and asks each what he is doing. The first says, "I'm digging a ditch." The second, being less a clod and aspiring to riches, says, "I'm making fifty cents an hour." Good pay in those days.

But the third laborer, a poet at heart, lifts his eyes to envisioned spires against the sky, and says with pride, "I'm building a cathedral!"

Then the lecturer would exhort everybody to see the wonder and the glory in the meanest of tasks, and great uplift prevailed.

I've been building a cathedral.

The sacred nature of the work inspires me, but I am not overwhelmed. I can see how building a cathedral is much like any profane construction, even as tedious as digging a ditch, but it has been fun—not just for me but for some others. You can believe that I was inveigled.

I have a cousin of many parts whom I have praised variously, and will not now praise again, and one of his many hobbies is making, repairing, and restoring new and old windvanes. So when the Episcopal church of St. John added an "undercroft" to its edifice in Thomaston, my cousin provided a gold-leafed windvane in the pattern of the Angel Gabriel, with which the parishioners were pleased and which was to be mounted on the new undercroft. It seems the weathercock, symbolic of the Three Denials, has long been the most popular pattern for church windvanes throughout Christendom, but Gabe, as my cousin calls him/her, is a close second. In his long and distinguished career Gabriel has been imagined all the way from a fine old gentleman with white beard and golden wings to a plump and bare-tailed cherub—and here and there a female. The horn is standard. Gabriel is the celestial messenger and public announcer, bringer of tidings, and he will tootle his tooter at the last hooraw. So time flew by, and this Gabriel windvane had not been put on the undercroft roof, and my cousin asked why. I inquired, and the vicar told me it would be architecturally rude to set Gabriel directly onto the roof, so a special cupola was planned as a proper pedestal for him but what with this and what with that the project was still in the future. Perhaps I would like to volunteer?

The "undercroft" is not really below ground, as undercrofts should be, but is fairly tall, and in Maine a cupola is always a kewp-pa-low. I agreed to make the cupola, and reduced the pitch of the roof to a drawing, keeping an ecclesiastical attitude consistent with the purposes. My cousin had done a superb job with Gabe, I should do as well. I cleared a place in my shop. I then went to a lumberyard and ordered eight hundred cubits of gophperwood and two hundred of shittim.

The job has gone along in that vein. Each morning I touch off my shop stove and add figure, strength, and beauty to my cathedral. It sits on two carpenter's horses. I accept my task as a challenge, because Thomaston is the town that went to sea and almost every house is a magnificent old ship-captain's mansion built by shipwrights in the days of sail, with gingerbread

and widow's walks and cupa-lows—curious and cunning crafts-
manship with which Gabriel's perch must forever compete. In
my town, which is not Thomaston, home workshops are geared
to lesser projects, like lobster traps, skiffs, stormsash. So what I
am doing has had attention from the neighborhood and some of
the jokers have said some amusing things. One morning I was
reminded that the scaffolding in the Sistine Chapel cost a good
deal more than they paid Michelangelo. Again, I was informed
that the basilica of Ste. Anne de Beaupré is intended never to be
finished, but workmen will continue to adorn and embellish forever. At least fifteen funny-ones have gazed in awe, feigned
respect, and then asked if I plan to put a centerboard to her?
And the man next door says if it turns out all right he'd like me
to make him fifteen beehives.

The vicar came to tell me he had made arrangements for a
crane to hoist Gabe's pedestal into place. I have epoxied the
spindle, and need to apply one more coat of paint. I have built
my cathedral and Gabe will announce the Thomaston winds,
fair and foul.

(Additional: Gabriel, horn into the wind, is in place on St.
John's undercroft in Thomaston.)

Before Television

Antique boutiques delight me only slightly, for I dislike to
see the commonplaces of my youth offered at many times
their fair prices, making me sad that I didn't save one of everything to grow old along with me. Think what I'd be worth today
if I'd kept a thousand buttonhooks. But rather than wait outside, I went into the old barn by the side of the road to look at

the junk, and there was a coal sieve full of stereoscope slides on top of a commode. The coal sieve and the commode are not, I think, objects d'art, and if they are I would appreciate a lucid explanation from an expert. The coal sieve was to reclaim unburnt cinders from the ashes, and the commode was to house the bed-chamber potty. But stereoscope slides belonged to culture, were television's grandfather, and were meant to cheat the time on rainy afternoons. "How much do you ask," I said to a young lady who was arranging shaving mugs on a what-not, "for the stereoscope slides?" She deigned to look over her shoulder more or less towards me, and said, "The what?"

"The stereoscope slides."

"You mean them pitchers there?"

"Yes, these pictures here."

"What did you call them again?"

The sweet thing, burdened so heavily with youth, had no notion of the purposes of the pictures, and when I asked if she had a machine (I thought "machine" would mean more to her than "viewer") she shook her head and looked about as if she hoped somebody would come and rescue her. She didn't know what the coal sieve was for, and she said a commode made a dandy liquor locker.

To be truthful, I'm not that old. The stereoscope had ceased to be important entertainment by my time, and as acquaintances of Fatty Arbuckle and Pearl White we youngsters looked through the family stereoscope in the parlor as an already oddity of the past. But we did have one, and it had been there in the parlor since it was new. I still have ours. And in my boyhood, almost every home had one on a parlor table, something out of date but not yet discarded.

There were three kinds of slides; a slide was a pasteboard backing with two pictures pasted side by each. The first two kinds were "boughten," or store-bought. One would be a general view of something like the Taj Mahal which would sell anywhere in the world. The second would be of a local scene, such as Mitchell's gristmill, and would sell in a town or an area. The third kind was homemade, and went for family pictures, scenes on the old farm. There were special cameras—Eastman made one—with double lenses, because the secret of the stereoscope was a double image that the lenses of the viewing-contrivance turned into three dimensions. It was an optical illusion, but when the card said "Scene in front of Brown's Store," the things in front of Brown's Store really were out in front.

The scenes of world-renowned places—Grand Canyon, Traflagar Square, Okefinokee Swamp—and the local views—Bijou Theatre, Mill Street Boarding House, New Steel Bridge—were always well labeled, with printing. But the homemade ones seldom got any identification, and after a few years had passed nobody quite remembered about them. You'd see two gentleman standing in front of a woodpile. "Who're they?" somebody would ask Grandpaw.

He'd come over, take the stereoscope, squint through the eyepieces, perhaps adjust the focus, and he'd say, "Gawd, I dunno. I think that might be the Bibber boys, but I wouldn't know which is which, now."

I didn't buy any cards from the young lady, nor did I want the coal sieve and the commode. She said they were asking a dollar apiece for the stereoscope cards, and I told her I thought that might be just about right.

If it is just about right. I've got a few thousand dollars tied up in stereoscope slides from the family plunder. The Matterhorn, Niagara Falls in winter, the Great Wall, the Bad Lands, the Bunker Hill Monument, Notre Dame de Paris, The Great Sphinx. Then Buker's livery stable, the old Whittier School, the Pinkham Shoe Shop, Ruggle's Boatyard, and Cutting Ice on Baglee's Pond. And, which are the ones I prize, pictures of two men standing by woodpiles. It's hard to believe the world once had little else to do.

Mistreated Indians

Some men are born with human rights, some have human rights thrust upon them, and some are just naturally happy. And it makes a difference who tells the story. Maybe you got excited at the stories in the newspapers about how the Indians are abused—our State of Maine Human Rights Commission went after the Down East blueberry growers for the deplorable housing provided for the Canadian Indians who come over the line to rake blueberries. Director Terry Ann Lunt-Aucoin cried out in anguish that the living conditions are "an abomination . . . a cruel exploitation of native Americans."

Behold! Robert and Lois McCauley (he's the snake man aforesaid) live in Bethesda, Maryland, and own five-six acres of saltwater frontage alongside us here at Friendship Back River. They do not have a cottage with much expensive stuff—just a piece of land—and they come to Maine every summer to tent out for a week or two. Dr. McCauley was important in the Department of HEW, and his wife was prominent in the affairs of a Baltimore museum. That is, educated, refined, well-to-do, it happens that they have no electricity at the Maine campsite, and consequently no running water, with open plumbing openly arrived at. They sleep on the ground in bedrolls. Their kitchen facility is a stone fireplace with open wood flame. They dig clams, jig for mackerel, hunt wild berries, and commune with nature. They love every minute, and look forward all winter to their next visit to Maine.

So Rob and Lois were here just as the awful news broke in

our papers that people were mean to the Indians. But without reference to that, Bob had just said, "Not everybody agrees with me, but for my taste the best sardine I can get down in Maryland is packed here in Maine by somebody named Wyman."

I said, "I've got a friend of long standing who'd greatly admire to hear you say that."

"Oh? Who's that?"

"State Senator down to Milbridge, name of J. Hollis Wyman. Owns the Jasper Wyman and Son Canning Company. He packs those sardines."

So lunches were put up, and the four of us made a day trip down to Milbridge, and Bob got a chance to tell Hollie that he packs a good fish. The sardine pack was over for the season, but the blueberry crop was coming in, and while the four of us were in his office, Hollie's telephone jumped in the air and he got his first call from the newspapers about this big abuse of the Indians. We listened while he parried the Associated Press, the United Press, the Bangor *Daily News*, and some others. The Human Righters had just let go a blast about the downtrodden Micmacs, the outraged Maliseets, and the persecuted Passamaquoddies. Hollie, swimming upstream, tried his best to explain. The Indians come of their free will, a year after year arrangement, and they arrive by families in trucks to stay in the "camps" provided by the food packer. These camps are tight frame buildings, equipped and ready. True, they sit on the blueberry barrens far from anything much, and they don't have electricity and they don't have plumbing. The Indians are well paid for raking berries, and by doing business with a chief rather than individuals, the processors spare themselves a lot of red tape. Until the Human Righters butted in, the annual deal with the Indian rakers was happy and serene. Indeed, after looking into the matter that particular summer, the Bangor *Daily News* editorialized that the Human Rights Commission had overstated, and had enflamed, divided, and antagonized through public utterance of over emotional rhetoric. Well said. Alexander Denny, chief of one tribe, comes with his wife and ten-year-old son and calls blueberry raking his "vacation." Chief Denny has a position with the Nova Scotian government, is important, and well off. Hollie told about another man who is a policeman in Canada, and wears his uniform while raking blueberries. Sabattus Nicholas, a Passamaquoddy, says he looks upon raking blueberries as "camping out," as a chance to restore age-old tribal lore of his ancestors. He says this explains why the Indians move the beds from the camps out under the trees, and also the cookstoves. His words suggested the camps which the Human Righters found abusive are not really all that bad. At least the Human Righters did overlook the truth that Down East real estate brokers can get up to three hundred dollars a month for just such camps, where out-of-state summer folks can enjoy a vacation worth going back home to brag about.

So we were sitting there and Hollie was on the phone defending his position, and the expression on McCauley's face was worth the day's trip. Hollie was shouting into the phone, "But, dammit! These Indians don't have to sleep on the ground!"

Bob turned to whisper, "And, dammit—neither do I!"

So there are ways and ways to look at Human rights, and we could see that Chief Micmac and Bob McCauley saw them one way, and Ms. Terry Ann Lunt-Aucoin saw them another.

The Whonkeroo

To cheer my day there came a letter from Don Seymore of Canton, New York, to ask about the Maine black flies. He says he plans a camping trip to Baxter State Park, and would like to know what sort of reception he will have from these insects. Don—you have certainly come to the right person. You will never get anything but the truth about black flies from me. Over the years our state publicity people have been enticing people with all manner of professional folders, and not one of them has ever mentioned the black fly as a tourist attraction. A good many of us deplore this conspiracy of silence, because the black fly is one of Maine's most talked about assets. He captivates the attention of visitors a good deal more than do our advertised attractions— our historical sites, our scenic views, our fine eating places. You'd think we had nothing but lobsters. But every summer thousands of people go home after pleasant Maine vacations, and they talk about nothing except the black fly.

Our Maine black fly remains in hibernation until approximately the time summer is officially opened by the Mount Katahdin Chamber of Commerce. This year summer is to be on the 12th, 13th, and 14th of July. Meanwhile, the black fly will stay clustered in hollow trees and caves, in a desultory manner. When temperatures moderate, he emerges in great flocks to perch in spruce trees as prelude to dispersing and foraging. The flocks sit on the branches, usually near a trunk highway, and often their gross weight snaps off the limbs, making cracking noises audible at considerable distance. As temperatures begin to warm they sing some, and then move about the state in swarms, taking up positions to await the arrival of tourists. The signal to attack is the arrival of the first Massachusetts driver.

Mr. Seymore will undoubtedly follow through with his camping plans, tent and sleeping bag and so on, but I, myself, would go camping at Baxter State Park by engaging a comfortable room at the Hermitage Motel in Millinocket. It is a good inn and has a fine dining room. The chambers are heated the year 'round. The management keeps the paths shoveled during the summer so the dining room is always accessible, and unless the guest wishes to hike in the woods there is no need to bring snowshoes. There is daily shuttle service to The Park by snowmobile, and frostbite and chillblain insurance is sold at the desk.

But if Mr. Seymore doesn't care to heed this good advice and does tent out in The Park, he may be lucky enough to see the annual "blind flight" of the black flies, which comes in late June just after the highway crews have taken down Frost Heave signs. It is an amazing spectacle. Entomologists have never given a lucid explanation of this strange flight, but the Indians had some folklore about it. They said that the great spirit of Mount Katahdin, Pamola, would rouse in his sleep at the season's first appearance of the black fly, and he would direct a mighty slap at the annoyance. This caused consternation in the flock, and whole populations of black flies would rise at once. Those on the north side of the mountain moved around to the south, and those on the south to the north. (This is done counterclockwise in alternate years.) The turbulence of the wind created by this tremendous swirl of insects will continue about the summit of the mountain for several days, and in the folklore of the region is known as the "whonkeroo." Woodsmen use the whonkeroo to tell time—did such and such happen before or after the whonkeroo? Thousands of people gather to behold this, and to hear the thunderous noise of the flight, but as the whonkeroo depends on the season a great many always come too early or too late. However, the sound of the flight can be heard afar off, and many who have not actually attended a whonkeroo are familiar with the heavy buzz over the region. Folklore says it is Pamola moaning in his sleep.

The Pamola myth about the whonkeroo is better explained by saying it is nature's way of protecting the genes, preventing inbreeding, and keeping the strain of the Maine black fly healthy and strong. It is, truly, a "blind flight" to separate the families and discourage incest. Otherwise, the Maine black fly would today be as docile and physically deteriorated as an Ontario mosquito or a Southern chigger.

The Wrong Day

A great many Mainers, and more every year, spend the winters in Floridy, which would be all right with me if they wouldn't send back their postcard snides about the salubrity of the weather. They might properly send cordial greetings saying, "Wish you were here" and let it go at that, but they always add, "Hope you're not buried in snow!" Here is the precise text of a card that came on a certain day: "Having fine time wish you were here. Hope you're not buried in snow so you can't get out. Keep the home fire burning and toss on another log for us! Bathing every day. Too bad you can't come down and enjoy our warm weather. Bye-bye."

When our chill factor hits bottom and Friendship harbor is frozen over, such levity is fine and can be excused and accepted, but what these jokers in Sunland never know is that 99 percent of such cards come on the wrong day. This one did. I'll tell you about Pete and Mildred:

Pete and Mildred had their "seasonal dwelling' here at Friendship for a couple of decades. It sits on a bluff of pointed spruce trees, looking down on the harbor and the Friendship lobster fleet, and you'd look a long time before finding a better spot. And as Pete and Mildred came each summer, they did some work to make their summer dwelling a year-round home to which they would retire.

So after a distinguished career in the Boston money business, Pete retired. They sold their lovely home in suburban Belmont, severed all ties, and came to Maine to settle in forever and see how many years it would take the selectmen of Friendship to get them off the "nonresident" list. ('Twas four, as I remember.) And as they were arranging their affairs to make the move, they got the usual flak from their Belmont friends and neighbors about the rigors of Maine and the wicked winters. "Why did you ever decide to go to *that* place!" The Belmont synonym for Friendship was "boondocks," and Pete and Mildred got a lot of boondocks. "Good place to go skiing, but . . ." And, "We'll be thinking of you when you're shoveling snow!" All on a par with the regular wisecracks on postcards from Florida. Pete and Mildred quietly explained they looked forward to their first Maine winter, said farewell, and moved to Friendship.

Their first Maine winter wasn't much one way or the other. We had some snow, but not much, and we had some chilly days. There came one magnificent morning when Pete and Mildred could hardly see the boats moored in the harbor for sea smoke. Sea smoke is a vapor that rises when cold air moves in over the warmer water, a kind of fog, and everything that morning looked like a fuzzy fairyland, softened to tease the imagination. And after a day of a magic casement opening on the forlorn, the wind shifted abruptly to southeast and a Bermuda air moved in to dissipate the sea smoke. Everything was clear again, and night settled over the quiet harbor. Then it rained warm water all night, taking away what little snow we had, and Pete and Mildred awoke to find everything had cleared and a dazzling sunrise commenced a rousing day that was just like July. But, you see, it was January. The way the sun set everything to shining and shimmering was incredible, and as they looked off during breakfast Pete and Mildred watched the fishermen push out in their skiffs, and in their shirtsleeves, to pump out their bilges after the rain.

So right after breakfast Mildred came from the kitchen to find Pete siting in the big chair, his feet on a hassock, looking entranced at summertime Friendship harbor in the depth of a Maine winter. He had a smile as if inwardly enjoying a private joke, and Mildred could see he was having deep thoughts. He looked like the cat that swallowed the canary.

"My, my!" said Mildred. "Don't we look smug this morning! What in the world has you looking so pleased with yourself?"

Pete didn't relax his smile one bit when he turned to look at her. He said, "I was just listening to the Boston radio."

Mildred said, "So?"

Pete said, "Belmont got twelve inches of snow last night."

That was the day I got that postcard from Florida, and as I say—sometimes they come on the wrong day.

Warm and Cozy

It would be tedious to enumerate all the reasons for holding the annual chimney fire precisely during the family Christmas festivities. Suffice one; we have established a tradition in this matter until this year everybody foresaw the holocaust when Uncle Terence tossed the wrappings from his new slippers into the fireplace, where our cheerful yule log was performing well and in no need of assistance. "Here it goes!" somebody said, and somebody else said, "The fire department number is on the red sticker!"

A chimney fire need not be a dangerous matter, and on Christmas it can be a jolly part of the program. Our chimney is new and sound, and the roof was covered with new snow that would help with a luster of midday to objects below except that the red glare was now mounting into the sky and alarming people all up and down the road. It was unlikely a spark would find a host and it was reasonable to suppose that in a few moments the soot would burn itself out and we could return to our gifties. "I think there's no need to worry," I said.

Then I telephoned to the fire department.

In more populated communities than ours, firemen remain in a nonsocial context, and when called arrive at many blazes where they have been not formally introduced. This is a shame, because a Christmas chimney fire offers a warmth that friends and neighbors can embrace better than strangers. On Christmas, it is better to cry Joyeux Noël! and hold the front door open for somebody you know and love. Now, the first fireman to arrive was accoutred and garbed with safety effects suitable for a space shot, and he could have been out of Central Fire Station in New York City. Had he been out of New York City I wouldn't have known him. I would have felt shy about holding the door while he came in with his extinguisher. But here, he was Dougie Richards, one of the Richards boys, and he'd been in and out of our house in nonconflagration sociability time and time again.

"Merry Christmas!" I said.

Behind Dougie came Wesley Lash, boatbuilder and nautical philosopher, and then Buddy Jameson, plumber and neighbor. Holiday remarks having been given and answered, they spoke not a word but went straight to their work, and after peeping up the chimney they opinionated that the fire had burned itself out. As I had said, there was no need for alarm.

Then we made Christmas cheer and had the pudding. It is an ancient English bag pudding, full of plums, and in our family, along with chimney fires, has been the traditional Christmas dessert since before good King Wenceslas looked out upon the feast of Stephen. It must be piped to the table while the brandy flames, and everybody marches behind. Dougie stopped with the hard sauce, but Wesley and Buddy had some of each, hard and soft. Some old goo-ood.

The fire engine had been left in our dooryard, lights flashing, and this caused a few people passing to stop in and ask if there might be something they could do. When the firemen drove off we called Happy Noëls after them and wished them hearty Christmas cheer. Our voices rang over the snow, and the Christmas lights twinkled on their neoprene weather gear. "See you next Christmas," Dougie shouted, and then he wound up the siren. But he let it die when the engine came to the main road, and we heard the boys exclaim as they drove out of sight, "Happy Christmas to all and to all a good night!"

Ice Cream Shot

B ack when our Maine legislature was pondering returnable containers—a sensible idea that finally passed—the issue got foggy with all the paid performers. The lovers of tin cans came in droves to tell us that litter up and down the highways is a wonderful thing for a state that nurtures tourism, and they told us the nickel-back is an evil thing. Made me think of the ice cream bucket and the evil influence it had on the morals and honor of the State o' Maine. The ice cream tub was a returnable, and it fostered an indigenous felonious tendency.

It certainly is improbable that tasty, rich ice cream would nurture crime. It was a Maine man who first put ice cream on a commercial basis, with a factory to provide it in wholesale quantities. In a few years, by catering to summer hotels, he built a business that went nationwide when other people saw what he was doing and imitated. This was long before mechanical refrigeration, so his enterprise depended on pond ice, rock salt, and a motor to turn the cranks. The Maine summer hotel, or resort, called a sporting camp, always went for the elegant. Guests paid well and expected the best. Ice cream, churned at home by hand, had not become common otherwise, but the sporting camps grabbed the chance and soon ice cream was the big thing for Sunday dinner. It was on the Friday, accordingly, that the steel containers of ice cream were packed in rock salt inside these wooden tubs and shipped from the factory. The Friday train was the ice cream train. But the ice cream would arrive on Saturday, and a stage from each camp, or a boat where needed, would be waiting at the station. These tubs were heavy, and each had two strong metal handles. Each would be waltzed to the platform, loaded onto the stage, and taken posthaste to camp so fresh ice could be applied to hold the ice cream stiff until Sunday dinner. Choreboys would have dug a cake of ice from the icehouse, and chipped it. Ice renewed, the tubs would wait until cook opened them to serve dessert.

Resorts could be rated by the number of tubs of ice cream arriving each week. A single tub meant vanilla and a low guest count. Two tubs (vanilla and chocolate) meant an average season. A place that took a third tub was booming, that was strawberry, and only the high priced camps took a fourth, which was tutti-frutti.

Camps tried to return the empty containers and tubs on the Monday. So after Sunday dinner the potwalloper would wash the containers, and the choreboy would take the tubs to the edge of the woods and dump out the salty icewater. And this is where outrageous crime rears its ugly head. Salt attracts deer, and thus every camp had a dandy salt lick on the fringe of the forest, to which the sportive deer repaired. Every vacationist took pictures of these lovely deer, pawing the ground and lapping and cavorting around in fine fettle. And the ice cream tubs would return to the creamery so more ice cream could come on the next Saturday and more salt added to the deer lick. Eastman Kodak paid lavish dividends as the sporting camps sold film for deer pictures.

Which was never illegal. Ice cream tubs had to be dumped somewhere. What was illegal was the "ice cream shot" after the summer visitors had gone home and the hunting season opened. True, the ice cream shot was never looked upon with favor as a right thing to take, and was rightly reserved as a last-ditch chance to get a deer for a paying guest who had not shot his own. A man from Philadelphia who expected to go home without his deer would be awakened at dawn by a rifle shot, and after breakfast would find a deer ready to go with him. The choreboy deserved a tip for waking him up, of course. And it made him more cheerful about presenting his check in full at the lobby desk. "Good trip home, Mr. Prindle! And see you next fall!"

Nobody in Philadelphia was told about the ice cream shot. But it goes to show how returnable containers can nourish corruption, deceit, and crime.

The Free Seeds

Roddy Tomkins spoke to me in the post office Tuesday morning, and articulated as follows: "I was readin' that pussyflage you wrote about plarntin' gardins an' how the volunteers would come, an' I thought for sure you was about to say suthin' about gittin' free seeds from congressman."

"Oh?"

"How come you di'n't?"

"Trade secret," I said. "If I tell you, you'll blab it all over, and everybody in town will start being a writer."

"Everybody in town *is* a writer," said Roddy.

"All right. Reason I didn't work in free seeds from congressmen is because I didn't think of it—but if I had thought of it, I still wouldn't of had if I did."

"Have had," said Roddy. "But why not?"

"Because it don't pay to shoot off all your fireworks in one big bang. Free seeds from congressmen gives me another installment. I could sit down and write one piece that would cover every subject, and then what would I do for next time? So I've got free seeds in reserve. Thanks for reminding me."

"My pleasure."

"How long would you say it was," I said, "that you got free seeds from a congressman?"

"Maybe about 1930. P'aps the depression had something to do with it. After that there Roosevelt got in we had a plague of Democrats, and I'm pretty sure I got my last seeds from a Republican. Name was Beedy, seems to me. Yes—Beedy. He was a lawyer, and worse than that—he came from Portland. I didn't vote for him, as I never voted for nobody from Portland. Being from Portland, he prolly didn't know a marigold from a banyan tree, but he sent me free seeds."

"Were they any good?"

"Pretty good. They come in little packages marked 'not for sale' and instead of coming to boxholder-local they come with my name and address on 'em. After Beedy, no congressman ever called me anything except boxholder-local. The government stopped being folksy when it quit the seed business. They's something about seeds makes everybody kin. I recall one year Beedy sent me some okra seeds. I di'n't know what okra might be and I still don't. Didn't sprout. All else come good, but I was some disappointed when that okra failed. Always wondered what it was."

"It's a mallow, grown for its edible mucilaginous pods—used in soups. Never does well here in Maine."

"Is that so? Don't say! Well, give Beedy credit—he tried. And I tried. I watched for okra sprouts clear'n up to the time the cucumbers was done, and the next election I broke my vows and walked three miles in a rainstorm to vote for Beedy."

I said, "I think Beedy served four terms in all."

"I guess so, but he got trimmed the year he stopped sending seeds. I guess nobody nowadays can appreciate how important them seeds was. People were feet-up at the kitchen stove, dawdlin' away the depths of Febu-wary, and the mailman would jingle up with the *Country Gentleman,* the interest notice from the bank, and a batch of seeds from the congressman. Put new life into everybody. I'd shove an armload of wood into the stove and sit there fondlin' them seeds and think about hoeing through a hot June. The country was in good hands. Congress was in touch with the farmer. Nawthin's been the same since."

"Don't you suppose the free enterprise seedsmen ganged up and lobbied against free seeds?

"Prolly. But you got to wonder about the intelligence of a congressman that will vote himself out of a good thing, and let the seed people take over the seed business. Shouldn't of done it."

"Shouldn't *have* done it."

"You write it your way and I'll speak it mine. Mucilaginous. So that's okra. I prolly wouldn't of liked it if the stuff did sprout on me."

"Prolly," I said.

Back River Hold

Deciding to spend some six hundred dollars for a new ten-inch bench saw, I telephoned the hardware store in the city and was put on "hold." Mr. Bagshot, it seems, was on another line. So I laid the telephone on the table and went up to the garden to hoe peas, thinking it could wait for Mr. Bagshot just as well as I could. That afternoon a truck came from the telephone company to find out why my phone was out of order, and the boy put it back on the cradle. That hold cost Mr. Bagshot six hundred dollars.

Thus it is. Our telephone is at the house, and I am not usually. My wife is adept at parrying, and usually takes care of people who want to talk to me. You'd do well to listen to her. But now and then somebody wants to know if she can't call me to the phone, and sensing some imminent amusement she sometimes says, "Well, yes—I suppose so." "All right—I'll hold!"

The game is afoot!

After she gains some control following the spasm of unlimited hysterics, she staggers through the front door to clang the ship's gong we have on the front of the house. The town is thus notified that I am wanted on the telephone. Fishermen at sea look up and smile. Choppers up on the hill hear the bell over the roar of chainsaws and nod their hard hats. Some poor soul is on hold.

There are people who believe in Hope, Purity, Motherhood, the Constitution, and the Telephone. I should be ashamed of myself. But nobody has ever been put on hold from my telephone unless he asked for it, and that makes a difference. However he feels about it afterwards, he should respect the fact that he has contributed a great deal of mirth and jollity to the good folks in my miles around. When my wife pounds that gong, they chuckle and chuckle.

Unbiased Survey

E very so often somebody asks who got surveyed. These public opinion polls and surveys go on all the time, and nobody ever knew of anybody who got polled or surveyed. It is accordingly amazing that we can be persuaded and guided and beguiled by a consensus that derives from nobody. We go along placidly through the decades, influenced and happy, taking for granted that because there was a public opinion poll, somebody got polled. Well, the other day I was surveyed.

It didn't happen just as I expected. I thought a gentleman with an identification button and a clipboard would push my doorbell and I would answer his questions while he put down Yes,

No, and Undecided. I would do my best to give the American people the benefit of my amazing erudition. But no gentleman came—it was a questionnaire in my R.F.D. box that I was to fill out and mail back. It had to do with Oriental affairs. I happen to be a dedicated non-filler-outer of any printed forms that do not carry ten years in jail and ten thousand-dollar fine, and in addition I have no opinions about the Orient except that I agree with William Jennings Bryan that we should not establish coaling stations in the Philippine Islands. I did not answer this survey nor did I mail it back. I am still unsurveyed.

Years ago in the heyday of radio, I did a morning wake-up show from the farm. The radio station in the city ran in a "loop," and every morning at seven I would push a button and devote fifteen minutes to piffle, trivia, and bosh. I had a big New Hampshire rooster that was always around the dooryard in the summertime, and with a few handfuls of corn I trained him to crow when I waved my hand. I'd liven up the radio patter by waving my hand. There was something about being a straight man for a rooster that I liked, and it wasn't common for radio stations to broadcast roosters. Shows you the kind of programming that went on. After I had been doing this broadcast about a year, the radio station hired a survey team to rate me and determine the extent of my "listening audience." In due time a report came, and we had statistical evidence that I was reaching 78 percent of the available listening audience. I felt good about this overwhelming popularity until I wondered what other kind of audience there might be.

Not only might be, but definitely was. The biggest audience at seven o'clock in the morning turned out to be the nonlistening audience. Very few people, it seemed, cared to tune in at that hour to hear a rooster crow. And the pollsters who derive statistics for radio stations ignore these oddballs judiciously. Radio stations hardly care to offer nonlistening listeners to the advertisers. So instead of broadcasting to 78 percent of a million people, my rooster and I were reaching 78 percent of 2 percent of them. My rooster wasn't so important as he thought. I decided any proper unbiased survey begins by deciding on which side it is best to be biased; that a pollster on his toes finds out first what his client wants to prove. This, snide as it was, led me to ask on the air that listeners who had been polled drop me a card or tingle the telephone. I repeated this every morning for two weeks, and got no response whatever.

It was at just that time that my congressman urged everybody to write to him or send him a telegram. He said, "We desperately need a strong expression of public opinion to offset and counteract the public opinion being generated by the opposition."

Which, no doubt, is the whole point. In my radio days some county agent somewhere said that playing radio music in a dairy barn had a soothing effect on bossy, and in relaxation she produced more milk. Mood music, I suppose. Well, our radio station played music except for my fifteen minutes of patter and cocky-doodle. So I got a letter from some farmer upstate who said that he had taken a poll, and while his cows certainly liked the music on the station, they all stopped chewing the minute I came on to catch every word I said.

I've seen nothing about the results of that Oriental poll. The rooster? I went off the air and we ate him. What good did 78 percent of the listening audience do him?

Not All Pure

T was either Kin Hubbard or Abe Martin who said February makes a dandy month to stay in the house and trace ancestors. If, like me, you're not that much of a family tree buff, February is still a good month to stay in the house. Tracing ancestry has certain surprises, I think, that confirmed ancestry tracers suppress. Long ago I told the story of Bill Goff, who walked down from Maine at the news of the Revolution and took part in the Battle of Lexington and Concord. During the excitement a Minuteman officer noticed him, and since he was not in uniform the officer asked him what company he was with. Bill, fired up with zeal, said, "I ain't with no company, I'm fighting alone!" The story is reasonably true, and Bill Goff was a real person.

Then I got a letter from a lady in the Far West who was making the most of February, and she was grateful to me. She had been filling out the family tree, and there was a vacant limb. She had searched and searched, but she had been unable to find anything about her great-grandfather, William Goff. But there she was, reading my little story, and up leaped her great-grandfather before her very eyes. Bill Goff! At the Battle of Concord! She couldn't begin to tell me of the fruitless hours she had spent in libraries trying to find Bill Goff. And thanks to me, she now had her lineage complete, and Bill Goff was in place as the father of her very own dear grandmother! Since she had enclosed postage for reply, I felt I owed this lady an answer, and I didn't know what else to tell her except the truth. That is, that Bill Goff didn't marry until he was a very old man, and he died without legal issue.

My beloved maiden aunt, who was our family's ancestry bug, found a couple of scoundrels that she soft-pedaled. One doesn't seem such a scalawag nowadays because he was merely drummed out of church for refusing to pay his pew rent. But in the 1600s this was very wicked, and he must have been a brave man to stand up to the authorities. I used to remind my aunt that Henry David Thoreau became something of a hero for not paying his tax, but Thoreau wasn't one of *us*, and that made some difference. Then there was a scoundrel who absconded from a bank with a boodle and went to Canada where he turned good and did well. But my aunt would change the subject. She felt only the good were worthy.

I used to think it would be fun to introduce that aunt to Captain Will Harding of East Brunswick. Captain Will used to take visitors through the old Harding mansion and show them the framed oil portraits of the Harding ancestors. Will was proudest of one that hung in the kitchen. It showed a fine-looking man in maybe his forties, pinky-cheeked, bright eyes, robust enough, and an expression of good chraracter and upright morals. He wore a velvet frock with silver buttons, with lace at the cuffs and at the throat. Captain Will would linger at this portrait, and then would say, "Remarkable man—pirate, you know."

Which he was.

So I would wonder if my maiden aunt, prompted by Captain Will's pride in his pirate, might break down and brag about her ancestor who robbed a bank. If that didn't bring her off one up, she had the pew rent heretic in reserve.

This aunt did suppress the word about Uncle Henry for a good many years. She was undone by a near-nephew who was closer to old Henry than she was, and who didn't share her distaste for the wicked. He, browsing, chanced upon a random reference to Uncle Henry and pursued that gentleman on his own. In time, he came to realize that this maiden aunt had known about old Henry all along, and had kept him under wraps. So this near-nephew quietly researched Uncle Henry in detail, and in time produced a monograph on the rascal that elevate⅃ him into family prominence. Uncle Henry, it seemed, had been a tippler of note, the operator of a saloon with questionable reputation, and an entrepreneur of numerous things too sticky to mention. He was also agent for the Maine Mutual Accident Insurance Company. It was his custom, now and then, to collect the premium on a policy and neglect to forward it to the main office. So long as there was no claim, there was no great cry, but one day a man had an accident and put in a claim. Uncle Henry's luck had run out on him.

This near-nephew did a thorough job. He came up with photocopies of the charges, the indictments, the sentencing, and the papers remanding Uncle Henry to the State's at Thomaston. Henry succumbed while still an inmate of that institution in 1885, with several years of his time yet to go. His death certificate completes the monograph. Uncle Henry died in February.

Indian Massacre

Back in 1925 Mr. Whetstone of Worcester, Massachusetts, was rudely abused, although innocently, by some State o' Mainers, and it is time his story be told so belated apologies may be made. It was a terrifying experience, even though Mr. Whetstone was a meek little man who took a fright easily. Nobody in town, then, knew much about him. He had appeared with a brass-fronted Model T Ford a few years back, and had applied to Ashley M. Pinkham, our real estate man, saying he would like to buy a remote piece of land with tidal frontage where he could be alone and indulge his hobby, which was painting pictures. He said he was connected with an abrasives firm, which is why we called him Mr. Whetstone. Coastal scenery was easy to come by in those days, and it wasn't priced too high, so Ashley soon had Mr. Whetstone fixed up with ten acres on Oyster Point. Oyster Point was remote enough, at the end of the road, a hairbrush of spruce trees that stuck out into Sebooksis Bay, and there was a house. It was a good house which had been built by an artist, so it had a studio with northerly light, big window, and Mr. Whetstone was delighted. He became a seasonal resident.

He didn't socialize, and only two people in town every got to know him: Ashley Pinkham, and John Wadleigh. Old John lived on the Oyster Point road, about a quarter-mile towards town from the Whetstone place, and Mr. Whetstone had asked him to keep an eye on his property in his absence and to stand by if any help were needed. He made it clear he was timid about being alone so far from town, and of course anxious about the house when he was in Worcester. So Old John became sort of a caretaker, doing some errands now and then but mostly watching on. He told people Mr. Whetstone was a fine man.

On this particular occasion, when Mr. Whetstone was abused, he had arrived from Worcester about two o'clock in the morning. This was about right for a Model T, leaving after supper, so he arrived late and planned to rise early to do some painting in the morning light. That he had a short sleep is important, since he might have been tired and on edge, unready to face what was about to occur. He had been painting several hours and the morning was well advanced when he became aware of a disturbance. There was the sound of firearms, guns blazing away.

In season, gunfire at Oyster Point is not strange; the duck gunners like the place. But this was in the waning days of June, and Mr. Whetstone couldn't imagine what was going on. He paused, brush dripping, to look out his big window, and while he could not yet see anything, the gunfire was followed by the rude, rough, and uncouth shouts of many people, as if in the excitement of panic, commotion, and disaster. Electrified by such in this remote and idyllic situation, stood bewildered Mr. Whetstone by his easel, and as he stood thus there unfolded before his very eyes as if in a theater, the following:

Six Indians in breechclouts and paint came into view on his beach, dragging with them three non-Indians, to wit: an elderly gentleman in a Pilgrim stovepipe hat, a lady who was screaming wildly, and a small child best described as a toddler. Just as this group came bounding from the woods onto the sand, another shot rang out and the No. 6 Indian let go a cry of agony and fell kicking to the beach, where he expired in full view of Mr. Whetstone.

Indian No. 1 now pulled a canoe from the bushes, thrust it into the tide, and Indian No. 2 slammed the toddler down into it and steadied the craft while Indians No. 3 and No. 4 subdued the screaming female by winding a blanket around her head. Then they hove her, too, into the canoe. Meantime, Indian No.

5 tomahawked the elderly gentleman, scalped him, and came running along behind with his bloody trophy to push the canoe off and jump in the stern. This all happened so swiftly that the canoe was beyond the scope of the window before Mr. Whetstone could bring himself to believe anything like this was happening. He realized that it was all most unusual for Maine in 1925.

He steadied himself against the studio wall for a catch-of-breath, rubbed his eyes, and wiped the cold sweat from his forehead. He looked again at the two corpses on the beach, fled, and came through the woods to the highway and the house of Old John Wadleigh, where he reported what he had seen.

That's about it. Had Mr. Whetstone not fled so soon, but had lingered at his studio window a bit longer, he would have seen Indian No. 6 arise from the sand in good health, laughing, to go over and assist the elderly gentleman in the Pilgrim hat to his feet. He would have seen the canoe return to the ken of the window and then come ashore. And seen Indian No. 5 return the scalp to the elderly gentleman, who then put it back on his head. And he would have seen Mrs. Delia Whittaker, with a clipboard, come from the spruces and walk down to the beach, talking to the group as she came, because Mrs. Whittaker was the author and director of the Fourth of July pageant. This pageant was an annual effort of the Bunganuc Historical Society. This year they were doing the Oyster Point Indian Raid and Massacre of 1625, just three hundred years ago. The elderly gentleman was the pastor of the Growstown Methodist Church, and the screaming woman was my math teacher.

I tell this story not only because it is amusing, but because it teaches that History, when it repeats itself, should be careful not to scare people. Mr. Whetstone remained jumpy for years.

Beauty Aid

That television commercial that shows the lovely hands of
Mrs. Jones of Schenectady, which are just like those of her
sixteen-year-old daughter, had me mixed up the first two or three
hundred times it invaded my privacy. I thought it was selling a
beauty aid; not so—soap! You, too, can have lovely hands if you
use Joopy, or Naxim, or whatever it is in the dishpan. When I
realized it was soap, I had pleasant thoughts about the commercial whimsy of combining household detergent and hand lotion
in the same handy, family-size, bottle. The thurible, therapeu-
tic, and cosmetic qualities of the dishpan require some thought.

I bought my emancipation long ago. When dishwashing
machines were first offered, the gimmick was that the drudge
(housewife, homemaker) would be released from a sordid task
and could spend more time at cultural things. Nothing was said
about the gentlemanperson concerned, who was I. From our
first meal in our newlywed nest, I had stepped to the sink when
she began to lave, and there would be a wiper laid out for me. I
was the assistant. We would stand there hip by jowl, looking
out the sink window at petunias now and snowdrifts then. By
the time she dumped the dishwater in the sink, I would have
the dried dishes stacked in the cupboard. In those barbarous
times, I recall, there was a soap shaker. It was a little wire cage
on a handle, and when any kind of soap became too small for
easy handling, she would tuck the residue into this soap shaker.
When the soap shaker was whipped about briskly in the warm
water in the dishpan, it set up a sud of a sort, and that was how

dishes got cleaned. Nothing wasted. After the soap shaker came flakes and powders and the era of Beauty at the Sink was upon us. So I told her that a dishwashing machine would free both of us for cultural pursuits, and I wrote a check. After that, I didn't touch a dishwiper for many years, and only when a bolt of lightning took our kitchen apart and shorted our dishwashing machine beyond recall. The insurance company took quite some time to decide if I had had the lightning come on purpose, and until a new dishwashing machine was installed we stood at the sink again, she washing and I wiping. When I stepped up the first time, there was the wiper laid out, and again we looked at the petunias. And since then, we haven't washed and wiped again, dishpanwise.

It wasn't until our son matured and married that I went back to wiping. His pa-in-law and I, expecting to become grandfathers together, began a series of July fishing trips into the Maine wilderness, and the great amount of gear that we carried to keep us in comfort and content included a bottle of dishwashing detergent. We have been privileged to use a good camp owned by one of the timberland companies, and it has a sink with a window to peer from, but little else in the way of urban refinements. After every meal, Bill and I wash and dry, Bill washing. We faithfully make the dishes ready for the next time, and as supper is our most plentiful feast we make more of a ceremony at evensong.

Supper, perhaps, has been a fresh, split salmon, taken just previously from the adjacent stream, fetchingly roasted over glowing coals, basted freely, and garnished lightly to be served on native watercress. We don't have a strawberry shortcake with every supper, but we do like to have one with salmon. It goes good. As we prepare this modest sustenance, the swallows are skimming the lake, the redwings are flashing in the rushes, a hooty-tooter is hooty-tooting to his mate in younder pine, and we see that a doe has brought her two fawns down to drink. The sun is about to set over the mountain, and peace is on every hand. From a distance, the waterfalls at the outlet dam rumbles background music. Beauty and serenity—there is not cark nor care. Bill frequently remarks, "Think of the millions and millions of people in this world who have no idea where we are!" The shadows have lengthened when the biscuits are browned, and the salmon has attained his ultimate perfection. After nourishment, we meditate and contemplate quite a while, and then we do the dishes.

Bill sets the dishpan in the sink and squirts in a squeeze from the plastic bottle of liquefied and saponified delight—Joy, or Dove, or Whoppo, or Swipe, or Whatever. They all seem about the same when squirted. We scrape the orts onto a stump to please the moosebirds, we lay the dirties in the pan, and then Bill dumps in a pailful of hot pondwater. Instantly, the Great North Woods smell just like any kitchen sink in any civilized household, and our illusion of being alone in a remote place is burst apart by something that rudely suggests Schenectady. The hoot owl has ceased, the swallows and redwings have perched. The sun has set. That soap has taken over, and the pleasant flavor and the unguent benefits so liberally advertised have become an evil and obscene menace in a sacred place.

But with the pretty pinkies of Mother and Daughter Jones in Schenectady in mind, I must admit that Bill does have the loveliest dishpan hands in Township 14, Range 6, West of the Eastern Line of the State of Maine.